OUR UNITED STATES GOVERNMENT

by Clairece Feagin

EDUCATIONAL DESIGN, INC.   EDI 295

About the Author

Clairece Feagin taught United States government to high school students through the Correspondence Division at the University of Texas in Austin for 20 years. She received her B.A. from Baylor University and Ed.M. from Harvard University. She writes curriculum materials for correspondence courses as well as for social studies text books.

Acknowledgments

Special thanks to the high school teachers who have read and commented on this text, especially Robert Franzetti of Crockett High School, Austin, Texas, and to my husband, Joe Feagin, Professor of sociology at the University of Florida, and Esidro Ortega for insights and helpful commentary. Thanks also to high school government students in University of Texas correspondence courses who constantly remind me of the wonderful resource our country has in its youth.

Our United States Government
ISBN# 0-87694-351-2
295

© 2000 Triumph Learning.
Triumph Learning, 136 Madison Avenue, 7th floor, New York, NY 10016

A Haights Cross Communications company

15 14 13 12 11 10 9

Table of Contents

To the Student 5

Introduction 6

Study Tips 7

UNIT A. OLD IDEAS FOR A NEW GOVERNMENT 9

1. Laws Are Written Down 10
2. People Share the Power of Government 15
3. People Elect Representatives to Run Their Government 18
4. If a Government Is Bad, People Have a Right to Change It ... 22
5. Government Must Be Fair to All the People 24

UNIT A Summary & Quiz 27

UNIT B. NEW GOVERNMENTS IN THE NEW WORLD 31

6. How Governments Start 32
7. Some Early Governments in the New World 35
8. The Road to Independence 42
9. What Does the Declaration of Independence Say? 47
10. New Governments for the New States 49
11. 13 Separate Governments Get Together 51
12. A New Constitution 54

UNIT B Summary & Quiz 59

UNIT C. THE U.S. CONSTITUTION 63

13. What Does the U.S. Constitution Say? 64
14. The Bill of Rights 67
15. Changing Constitutions 71

UNIT C Summary & Quiz 75

UNIT D. THE LEGISLATIVE BRANCH OF GOVERNMENT 79

16. Lawmaking in Local Governments 80
17. Lawmaking in State Governments 83
18. How Laws Are Made in State Legislatures 86
19. Lawmaking in the Federal Government 19
20. How a Bill Becomes Law in the United States 94

UNIT D Summary & Quiz 99

UNIT E. THE EXECUTIVE BRANCH OF GOVERNMENT 103

21. The Executive Branch of Local Governments 104
22. The Executive Branch of State Governments 106
23. The Executive Branch of the Federal Government 108
24. Electing the President 113

UNIT E Summary & Quiz 121

UNIT F. THE JUDICIAL BRANCH OF GOVERNMENT 125

25. Courts and Cases 126
26. State Courts 130
27. Federal Courts 132
28. Supreme Court Decisions 136
29. Checks and Balances in the Judicial Branch 139

UNIT F Summary & Quiz 141

UNIT G. THE PEOPLE AND THE GOVERNMENT 145

30. Influencing Your Government 146
31. Paying for Governments 151
32. Influences on Your Political Beliefs 155

UNIT G Summary & Quiz 157

UNIT H. ANOTHER GOVERNMENT TODAY 161

33. Britain 162

UNIT H Summary & Quiz 166

Glossary 168

Index 171

To the Student

Dear Student:

Even though I will probably never meet you, I really care about your passing this course. In fact, I care so much that I've written this book especially for you.

Not long ago I was talking with a friend who is about your age. He was trying very hard to understand a textbook. I asked him how he liked the book—if he thought it was a good one or not.

My friend thought a bit, then he said, "I guess it's ok. But it just has too many words."

A lot of students probably feel this way about their textbooks. Maybe even about their government textbooks! So I decided to write a government text with fewer words. Here it is.

I've tried to use clear words in this text —words which will help you understand what your government is all about and also help you pass this course. I hope you enjoy using this text.

Clairece Feagin
Austin, Texas

Introduction

This is a book about government—**your** government.

 Government *is a way of making decisions.*

In this book you will learn

- Where your government came from,
- How your government works,
- How you and every other citizen can have a part in **your** government.

The United States government did not just happen. It took a lot of work by a lot of people over many years to create the government we have today. Our government has continued to grow and change during all of its more than 200-year life.

To stay strong and free, the U.S. government must continue to change as the people's needs change. But changes should not "just happen." They should be made by voters who are well informed—voters who understand the problems the country faces, voters who can make intelligent decisions about the answers to these problems.

You are, or soon will be, of voting age. As a voter, you **can** have a part in how the government of the United States is run. Understanding how the government works will influence your vote. **Not** understanding how the government works will also influence your vote—you'll vote in the dark.

As you read this book, remember:

It takes a lot of work by a lot of people to run a country. Every voter's opinion is important.

- Learn how the system works.
- Learn what is going on.

> **Your vote can express your opinion.**
>
> **Make your vote count.**

Study Tips

This book is divided into eight Units. As you study each Unit, the following steps will help you do your best.

1. Read the **Learning Objectives** and the **Introduction** for the Unit.

2. Read each chapter as it is assigned. Think about what you are reading.

3. Answer the questions in each **Think About It** section.

4. Now read the chapter again.

5. After you have studied each chapter, you should be able to do the True/False **Unit Quiz** at the end of the Unit very easily.

6. Study any questions you may miss on the **Unit Quiz** after your teacher grades the quiz. Re-read any parts of the Unit which have given you trouble.

7. You should now be ready for the **UNIT TEST** which your teacher will give you.

Happy Studying!

Learning Objectives for Unit A

When you have finished this unit, you will be able to:

- State what a law is.

- Explain why people need laws.

- Explain why laws should be written down.

- Give examples of laws which say what people *may* do, what people *may not* do, and what people *must* do.

- State what government is.

- Explain why people have governments.

- Explain the differences between these systems of government—**anarchy**, **monarchy**, **dictatorship**, **direct democracy**, and **representative democracy (republic)**.

- Name important documents from England which influenced the U.S. system of government.

- Match important ideas from the past which became a part of the new U.S. government with the places from which these ideas came.

- List important ideas about government which the English settlers brought with them to the New World.

UNIT A — OLD IDEAS FOR A NEW GOVERNMENT

1776

1776 is a year most Americans have heard about. It was the year that the 13 English colonies in North America decided to become **independent**—that is, to stop being colonies of England and become a new nation on their own.

This new nation became the United States. The government of this new nation was different from that of any other nation in the world. It gave the people more freedom than any government ever had.

Where did the ideas for the new government come from?

Did the people who formed the new government think of new ideas all on their own? Or did they use ideas which others had used in the past?

Most of the ideas which became a part of the U.S. government were not new. They had grown slowly over many centuries.

The **new** part of U.S. government was the special way in which many **old** ideas were put together.

Five Ideas from the Past

- Laws are written down.
- People share the power of government.
- People elect representatives to run their government.
- If a government is bad, the people have a right to change it.
- Government must be fair to all the people.

All of these ideas became a part of the U. S. system of government. These ideas are very important to Americans today, but they did not start in the United States. Each of these ideas was started by someone long ago. But most governments didn't follow them.

The people who formed the U.S. government knew about these old ideas and believed they were good. So they decided to make these ideas part of the system of government in the United States. The United States was the first country to use all these ideas in its government.

In this Unit, you will learn where each of these old ideas started.

Laws Are Written Down

What Is a Law?

 *A **law** is a rule made by a government which people must obey.*

Laws tell people what they may do, what they may not do, and what they must do.

Why Do People Need Laws?

Laws
- protect people and their property and
- help keep order.

Tony's Band

Tony's band was on tour. They had been playing together for almost a year now, and they were sounding really good.

This was the band's first real tour, and so far everything was going great. Their van had only broken down once, everyone was getting along, Tony's new songs were a hit, and the band was even making pretty good money.

It was Joe's turn to drive. The others settled back for a little sleep before they pulled into San Miro for their next concert.

Suddenly the boys woke up as the van screeched to a stop. Joe was yelling, "What's going on?" Outside the van was the worst traffic mess they had ever seen.

The cars didn't seem to be in any order. Some kept to the right; some kept to the left; and some drove right down the middle of the road.

Motorcycles and bicycles were darting in and out between the mess of cars. And the boys didn't see a stop sign or a traffic light anywhere.

"This place is weird," Tony thought.

"We'll never get anywhere in this mess," Joe was yelling.

"Stop at that cafe and let's eat," Fred said. "I'm starved."

"Yea. And maybe when we're done, all these cars will be gone," John added.

Joe parked the van, and the boys went inside the cafe. While they were waiting to order, Tony looked out the window. Two guys were breaking into their van. One of them was taking out the boys' guitars.

Tony and the others jumped up and headed for the door, bumping into a waiter as they ran.

"Call the cops," Tony shouted to the waiter. "Those guys are ripping off our guitars."

"We don't have any cops in San Miro," the waiter said.

"No cops?" Tony turned and looked at the waiter, not believing what he heard.

"Who makes people obey the law?"

"We don't have any laws in San Miro," the waiter told him.

"No cops. No laws. No guitars. No concert. No band." Tony thought.

When Tony reached the van, Joe and Fred and John had chased off the thieves.

"They don't have any laws in this place," Tony yelled to the others. "And they don't have any cops here, either."

The boys got into the van, and Joe started the engine. As he pulled out of the parking lot, the traffic mess looked even worse than before.

"I say we hit the road!" Tony said. "Our van will either get totaled, or our guitars will be ripped off."

"Fine with me," Joe said. The others agreed. Cops and laws might be a problem sometimes, but with laws, at least you know what you can expect.

You are probably thinking, *"How could there be a place with no laws? San Miro couldn't be real. Tony must have been dreaming."*

You may be right. Maybe Tony was dreaming. But asleep or awake, Tony knew he didn't want to stay in a place with no laws.

In a place with no laws, people could do anything they pleased. There would be confusion and disorder. There would be no way to stop people from doing things which hurt other people.

Governments make laws for everyone in the group. With laws, people know what to expect of each other.

Think About It

1. Would you like to live in a place like San Miro? Why or why not?
2. Why do people make laws?
3. What is a law?
4. Name three laws which controlled what you did or did not do this week.

How Do People Know What the Law Is?

In some countries, laws are written down. The law is the same for everyone, and everyone can know what the law is. If the lawmakers change the law, everyone is told about the change. When the leaders of the government change, the system of laws stays the same. New leaders may make new laws, but the way laws are made does not change.

In some countries, laws are not written down. The people who rule make their own laws. These laws may not be the same for every person. These laws may not even stay the same every day. The rulers may change the laws at any time they feel like it. They don't even have to tell the people when they change the laws. When new rulers take over the government, they may change all the laws if they want to.

What Are the Rules?

Maria was on her way to school when her mother's car broke down. Maria got to school 30 minutes late. Mrs. Porter gave Maria a mean look and made Maria stay after school for one hour.

11

Tom went to the late movie. When his alarm clock rang the next morning, he was too sleepy to get up. He turned off the alarm and went back to sleep. It was noon when he got to school. Tom's teacher, Ms. Mays, just said, "Try not to be late again, Tom." She didn't make Tom stay after school.

As Mike was riding his motorcycle to school, he rode past the donut shop. He smelled the donuts and felt hungry, so he stopped to eat breakfast. He got to school 30 minutes late. Mr. Greer made a mark in his grade book and made Mike stay after school 10 minutes.

That night, Maria and Tom went to a party. Mike and Sue were there, too.

Sue said, "Hi, Maria. I didn't see you at band practice today after school. Where were you?"

"I had to stay an hour after school because I was late this morning," Maria answered.

"You must have been awfully late," Mike said. "I was late, too; but I only had to stay 10 minutes after school."

"I wasn't very late," Maria answered. "Only 30 minutes. But the rules here are very strict."

"That's funny," Mike said. "I was 30 minutes late, too. Maybe Mr. Greer just likes me!"

Tom felt his face getting red. He turned and went to get another soda.

"Is everyone going to the game in Plainfield next weekend?" asked Sue.

"I wouldn't miss it," Maria said.

"Are you going to the Plainfield game?" Tom asked as he came back to the group. "I'd like to go, but I don't know if Dad will let me have the car."

"You don't need a car," Mike told him. "The school bus is going. It only costs $2."

"School bus?" Tom asked. "Are you sure?"

"Mr. Jackson told us this morning," Sue told Tom. "Weren't you listening?"

Tom's face turned very red. "I wasn't at school this morning," he said. "I overslept."

"How late were you?" asked Mike.

"Noon," Tom said. "I got to school at noon."

"I guess you'll be staying after school for about a week!" Maria laughed.

"Uh, no," Tom said. "Ms. Mays didn't say anything about staying after school."

Maria gave Mike a puzzled look. "I thought the rules here were very strict!" she said.

"I think we should find out," Mike answered.

The next week Maria went to see Mr. Jackson, the principal.

"What's the rule here when a student is late?" she asked. "Could I please see the rule book? I'd like to read that rule."

"We don't have a rule book at our school," Mr. Jackson told her. "No one has ever written down the rules. It's just up to every teacher to decide what seems best."

Think About It

1. If you were Maria, how would you feel?
2. What changes would you make in the system of rules at Maria's school?
3. How do students at your school know what the rules are?

Government by People or Government by Laws?

Think how life would be with no laws which were written down.

- How would you know what you could do?
- How would you know what you could not do?
- How would you know if you had broken a law?

One day a police officer or a judge could use one law. Another day, a different law could be used. You would never know what to expect.

Hammurabi to the Rescue!

Long ago there were no written laws. Decisions were made by the person in power. Sometimes the decisions of the ruler were fair; sometimes the decisions were not fair. The people never knew for sure what they could do or what they could not do. The people never knew for sure what the punishment would be if they did something their ruler didn't like.

The first written laws we know about are more than 4000 years old. They came from the Middle East, from cities in what is now the country of Iraq. The most important of these laws were written by a king of the city of Babylon. His name was Hammurabi. About the year 1790 B.C. he had his laws chiseled on giant pieces of stone.

Everyone in Babylon could go to the stones and read the laws. The people could know the laws, and the judges could know the laws. The laws chiseled on the stones told the people what they **could** do and what they **could not** do. And the laws told what the punishment was if someone broke a law.

Since everyone knew what the laws were, the judges had to treat everyone the same.

These laws from ancient Babylon are called the **Code of Hammurabi**. Some of these pieces of stone still exist today.

The laws of our U.S. government are written down. We got this idea from King Hammurabi of Babylon.

Why should laws be written down?

Laws should be written down so people

- know what they **may** do, what they **may not** do, and what they **must** do.
- know what the punishment is if they break a law.
- are all treated the same.
- know what to expect of each other.

Think About It

1. What is a law?
2. What idea did our U.S. government get from King Hammurabi of Babylon?
3. Would you rather live in a place ruled by law or a place where the people in power make their own

Different Kinds of Laws

Some Laws Say What You May Do

You may vote when you are 18 years old.
You may run for Senator when you are 30 years old.
You may drive 65 miles per hour on many major highways.
You may have a jury trial if you are accused of a crime.

Some Laws Say What You May Not Do

You may not park your car by a fire hydrant.
You may not smoke in an elevator.
You may not murder anyone.
You may not steal.

Some Laws Say What You Must Do

You must pay income tax if you earn a certain amount of money.
You must have a driver's license to drive a car.
The police must have a search warrant to search a place.
The court must tell a person why he or she was arrested.

Think About It

1. Name one law which says what someone **may** do.
2. Name one law which says what someone **may not** do.
3. Name one law which says what someone **must** do.

CHAPTER 2

People Share the Power of Government

Who Makes the Rules?

You probably would agree that people living in a group need some rules for their behavior.

Think of some rules which control what you do every week. One rule says that people of a certain age must go to school. Another rule says that you must have a license to drive a car. Still another rule says that when you buy certain things at the store you must pay a sales tax.

Who makes these rules?

You also have rules in your school. One rule may be that you must get to your classes on time. You have rules for how to behave in the classroom or on the school bus.

Your school also has rules about **who makes** the rules and decisions for the school.

- Does the principal make all the rules and decisions?
- Do the teachers help make the rules and decisions?
- Do the students help make the rules and decisions?

Two Teams

Team A

Central High always had a good boys' basketball team. They had never won the state championship, but almost every year they won more games than they lost.

Coach Roberts knew a lot about basketball. He had played on the varsity team when he was at State University. He was a good coach, tough but fair, and the students liked him.

Coach Roberts made all the decisions for the team. He even chose the captain. The team members usually liked the coach's choice, but they thought that they should have a say in this decision. After all, it was their team.

Team B

Martha and Deneen were seniors. They had played basketball at Central High for three years. This year, both girls wanted to be captain of their team.

The girls' basketball team came close to winning state championship last year. Everyone hoped that this year the championship would be theirs.

The team had strong players and a good coach. All they needed was plenty of spirit and determination.

Both Martha and Deneen felt that they could give their team the leadership it needed to win. It was up to all the team members to decide which girl would be captain.

Tomorrow the team members would vote. Martha and Deneen were both very excited. Both girls agreed, however, that no matter who won, they would still be friends. Both agreed to work for the good of the team. After all, it was their team.

Governments Make Laws

You have learned why laws are needed. Laws help keep order. Laws tell people how they may behave. Laws tell people what they can expect from other people.

Someone must make the laws, and someone must enforce the laws. Someone must decide who has broken a law. Someone must make all the day-to-day decisions about what goes on in the group.

Laws and other decisions for a group of people are made by the government.

Remember: **Government** is a way of making decisions.

Different Forms of Government

Every country has a government. No two governments are exactly alike. In different forms of governments the decisions are made in different ways. Sometimes the decisions are made by one person. Sometimes the decisions are made by a group of people.

Here are some different forms of governments. The decisions are made in different ways in each of these.

Anarchy. Anarchy means "no leader." Anarchy really means that there is no government. All the people are free to do as they please. There are no rules. This situation has never existed in the real world for very long at a time.

Monarchy. A monarchy is a government in which one person is the ruler. This person is known as a **monarch**. A king or queen is a monarch. So is an emperor or empress. Monarchs have power because they are born into a ruling family. When one monarch dies, someone else from the same family becomes the new monarch. Until recently, in a monarchy, a monarch made all the decisions. Today, however, many monarchs have almost no power at all.

Dictatorship. A dictatorship is a government in which the decisions are made by one person. This person is known as a **dictator**. Dictators rule as they please. They usually do not care what the people want. Dictators often get their power by force.

Democracy. A democracy is a government in which the people share in making the decisions. The people decide who their leaders will be. This is generally done by voting for the leaders.

Direct Democracy. In a direct democracy, all the citizens take part in making the decisions and running the government. The group of "citizens" does not always include all of the people, however. "Citizens" might include only the men, or only the adults. In the old days, if a country had slaves, "citizens" would include only the free people.

Representative Democracy. In a representative democracy, the citizens elect a few people to run the government for them. The representatives make the decisions. If the citizens do not like what their representatives do, they can elect new ones.

> **Republic** is another name for a representative democracy.

An Idea from Ancient Greece

In a **democracy** the people make the decisions.

> Remember: **Democracy** means **rule by the people.**

In the United States today, we have a **democracy**. The idea of democracy comes from ancient Greece.

In ancient Greece, each city and the farmland around it was a separate small nation. They were called **city-states**, but they were actually tiny countries. Each city-state had its own government.

More than 2500 years ago, the people of some of the Greek city-states revolted against their dictators and set up democracies. The people of a city-state formed an **assembly** to run their government.

All the free adult men of the city-state were members of the Assembly. This left out a lot of people. Women could not be in the Assembly. Slaves could not be in the Assembly. Not even young men could be in the Assembly. Still, more people took part in running the government of these Greek city-states than in the government Greece had before.

The Greek city-states were small. They were so small that all the free adult men could take part in the government. This was called **direct democracy.**

Think About It

1. What does government mean?
2. How were decisions made for *Team A* at Central High?
3. How were decisions made for *Team B* at Central High?
4. Which team do you think had the better way of making decisions? Why?
5. Name five forms of government.
6. In which forms of government do the people have a say?
7. Which form of government do you think is best? Why?

CHAPTER 3 *People Elect Representatives to Run Their Government*

An Idea from Ancient Rome

The Greek city-states were not the only democracies in the ancient world. Democracy was also practiced in ancient Rome before the days of the Roman emperors. But Rome was much larger than a Greek city-state. Rome was so large that direct democracy was not possible, so the Romans elected a few people to run their government for them. This is called a representative democracy.

Representative democracy means that a few people speak and act for the whole population. All the people do not take a direct part in making the rules and running the government.

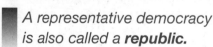 *A representative democracy is also called a **republic.***

In a representative democracy, all the voters have some say in the government when they elect their representatives. If the voters do not like the actions of their representatives, they can elect new ones.

The United States Today

Almost all the governments—city, state, and federal—in the United States today are representative democracies. The United States is too large for direct democracy. We elect a few people to make our rules and run our governments for us.

VOTING BOOTH
In the United States, people elect their own government representatives. Which ancient civilizations influenced this form of government?

The Federal Government

The federal government, which runs the country, is a representative democracy. The representatives we elect to run our federal government meet in Washington, D.C., to handle all the business of our nation's government. Washington, D.C., is our nation's capital. The leaders of our federal government make decisions for the whole country.

State Governments

The state government in each of our 50

states is a representative democracy. The people in each state elect representatives. These representatives meet in the state's capital to make the laws and carry on the business of the state's government.

Local Governments

Almost all the local governments in the United States are representative democracies. People in each city or county elect representatives to handle their local government's business.

In New England, some town governments are still direct democracies. In these towns, the people have town meetings and everyone can participate directly in running the town's business. But direct democracies are very rare today.

Think About It

1. What idea about government did we get from ancient Greece?
2. What idea about government did we get from ancient Rome?
3. Is the U.S. today more like the government of ancient Greece or ancient Rome? Why is this the case?
4. Where is our nation's capital?

An Idea from the Iroquois Nation

More than 400 years ago, the five tribes of the Iroquois Indian Nation had a representative democracy. The Iroquois (EER-uh-kwoy) Nation lived in what is now the state of New York. The five tribes of the Iroquois Nation were the Senecas, Cayugas, Onondagas, Mohawks, and Oneidas. In 1722, the Tuscarora tribe joined these other five tribes. After that, they were known as the Six Nations.

Village Councils

Each village of each tribe in the Iroquois Nation had a representative council which ran its government. All the representatives were men, but the representatives were chosen by the women of the tribes.

When a village council met to make decisions, each member of the council could give his opinion. He was allowed to speak as long as he wished. All the other members of the village usually came to the council meetings. They came to watch and to listen to what their representatives said. In this way they could know if the representatives were doing a good job. If a representative didn't do a good job of representing his people, he could be removed. A new representative would then be chosen.

Tribal Councils

Each tribe of the Iroquois Nation also had a tribal council. The tribal council worked just like the village councils. The women of each tribe chose men to be representatives to the tribal council. When the tribal council met, the members spoke about their views. Other members of the tribe came to the meetings of the tribal council to watch and listen to what their representatives said.

19

Confederacy Council

Together, all the tribes of the Iroquois Nation formed a strong group. They acted together in matters that were important to all the tribes. This kind of grouping is called a **confederacy.** The Iroquois confederacy had a **Confederacy Council** which made decisions for the entire nation. Each tribe sent representatives to the Confederacy Council. The Senecas sent 8. The Onondagas sent 14. Altogether there were 50 representatives in the Confederacy Council. But each tribe had only one vote. And all the tribes had to agree before any decision could be made.

If a representative didn't do a good job of representing his people, he could be removed. A new representative would then be chosen.

When the members of the Confederacy Council met to make decisions, each member could speak as long as he wanted to about his views.

Usually many people from all the tribes came to the meetings of the Confederacy Council. They came to watch and listen to what their representatives said. They knew that the decisions which their representatives made would affect their own lives. They wanted to know what the decisions were. And they wanted to be sure their representatives were doing a good job.

Think About It

1. How was the government of the Iroquois Nation like the government of ancient Greece? How was it different?
2. How was the government of the Iroquois Nation like the government of ancient Rome? How was it different?
3. How was the government of the Iroquois Nation like that of the United States today? How was it

What Form of Government Is This?

Case 1

The people of Weston need a new fire station. The mayor of Weston calls a town meeting to be held in the Town Hall. Most of the townspeople come to the town meeting. For almost three hours different townspeople give their views about whether a new fire station should be built.

They also talk about where the fire station should be built, who should build it, and how much money should be spent. Finally a vote is taken.

Case 2

The people of San Pedro also need a new fire station. The local newspaper has carried many stories about this need. Some people agree that a new fire station should be built. Other people think that the city cannot afford a new fire station.

The five San Pedro City Council members have each received hundreds of letters explaining people's views. Next week the City Council will meet to vote on this issue. It will then be decided if San Pedro will have a new fire station or not.

Think About It

1. Which of the above towns has a direct democracy? a representative democracy?
2. What form of government does your city or town have?
3. Name one issue which your city or town government has dealt with recently.
4. Name some ways in which people in your city or town had a part in the decision which was made.

CHAPTER 4

If a Government Is Bad, the People Have a Right to Change It

Ideas from England

In this section, you will learn how the government of England slowly changed from a monarchy in which the king had all the power to a government in which the people share the power.

You are probably thinking, *"I must have the wrong book. I thought I was studying U.S. government. First I read about King Hammurabi of Babylon. Then I read about ancient Greece and Rome, and about the Iroquois Indians. Now I am reading about England. What about the United States?"*

Here is your answer.

The U.S. form of government grew out of English government. The 13 colonies in the New World were settled by English people. Their ideas about government were based on the English system of government.

In their new home, the colonists wanted to have all the rights for self-government which people in England had struggled for centuries to get. They believed that this was their right.

A Powerful Monarch

At one time, the monarch in England had a great deal of power. But the nobles also had a great deal of power. They didn't want to lose any of their rights or give up their own power to the king.

Usually, when the king made a law, everybody had to obey. If a king wanted more money and soldiers to fight a war, he could order the nobles to pay more taxes and send more men.

In the early 1200s, King John did just this. He was fighting a war, and he told the nobles to send money and soldiers. But he asked for more money and soldiers than the nobles thought was fair.

The Nobles Speak Up

The nobles did not like the king to have so much power. They believed that they had a right to help decide how much tax money they paid and how many soldiers they sent to fight the king's wars.

In 1215 A. D., the nobles forced King John to sign an agreement. The agreement was called the **Magna Charta** (MAG-nuh CAR-tuh).

Magna Charta means **Great Charter,** a *charter* being a written contract.

The Magna Charta gave the nobles a share of the power of government.

The Magna Charta said:

- The king must treat all the nobles fairly.
- The king must consult the nobles when he wants to raise taxes.

The Magna Charta was written to protect the nobles. But even the common people were given some rights. The Magna Charta said:

- No free man could be arrested or put in jail unless a law permitted it.
- No free man could have his property taken away unless a law allowed it.
- Any free man was free to move about the country as he wished.

King John signed the Magna Charta. But later he refused to follow it. He said that because he had been forced to sign it, he did not have to obey its rules.

But with the Magna Charta, an idea had been born. A precedent had been set. A step toward democracy had been taken.

*A **precedent** (PRESS-i-dent) is a decision which is later used to help make similar decisions.*

Example: Your parents let you drive the car when you were 15. When your brother is 15, he will expect to drive, also. Your parents' decision to let you drive at age 15 was a *precedent*.

More Advice for the King

Fifty years after King John signed the Magna Charta, the nobles still felt that the king had too much power. The king would not listen to the nobles. So the nobles decided to get some help. They asked for support from church leaders, knights, and even the common people.

The nobles organized a group to give advice to the king. They called their group **Parliament**.

*The word **parliament** means a government meeting at which people talk things over.*

In England, the first **Parliament** was the group of people who met with the king and told him the views of the people.

At first, Parliament only talked with the king and told him how the people felt. Sometimes the king would listen. More often, the king would ignore the advice of Parliament.

Very slowly Parliament gained more power. But it was more than 400 years before Parliament had enough power to pass laws which the king would not ignore.

Today, Parliament runs the government of England. It is controlled by the common people, not the nobles.

Think About It

1. Why were the nobles upset with King John?
2. Why did the nobles force King John to sign the Magna Charta?
3. Did King John follow the Magna Charta? Why or why not?
4. Why is the Magna Charta important to us today?
5. Why did the nobles start the English Parliament?

CHAPTER 5

Government Must Be Fair to All the People

The English Bill of Rights

In 1689 Parliament wrote a Bill of Rights. It was approved by the king and queen. The English Bill of Rights put limits on the power of the monarch. It also protected the rights of the people.

The English Bill of Rights made the following rules:

- Monarchs can rule only if Parliament gives them this right.
- Anyone who is accused of a crime has the right to a trial by jury.
- People can petition the government if they believe the government has treated them unfairly.
- No punishment may be cruel or unusual.
- Fines for breaking the law must be fair.
- The monarch must follow the laws made by Parliament.
- Parliament must approve all taxes.

It had taken many centuries for the English people to get their rights. Now the people helped run the government. The people helped make the rules. The king did not have all the power. The people were very proud of their rights. They did not want anyone to take these rights away.

In the New World

When English settlers came to the new world, they brought their ideas about government with them. They remembered how life had been when the king had all the power. They remembered how long it had taken for the people to get a share of the power. In their new homeland, the settlers wanted all the rights which they had gained in England. The ideas about government which the English settlers brought with them became a part of the government of the United States.

Think About It

1. What ideas about government did we get from England?
2. Why is the English Bill of Rights important to us in the United States today?
3. Name four rights which the English Bill of Rights gave to the people.
4. What provisions in the English Bill of Rights are the same as rights you know about in the United States today?

Time Line for Unit A

1790 B.C. — *Code of Hammurabi*

King Hammurabi of ancient Babylon had a set of laws chiseled on giant pieces of stone.

600— 400 B.C. — *Direct Democracy in Ancient Greece*

The people of ancient Greece set up direct democ racies. All citizens (free adult males) could take part in running the government.

509— 31 B.C. — *Representative Democracy in Ancient Rome*

The people of ancient Rome set up a representative democracy. The citizens (free adult males) elected a few people to run their government for them.

A.D. 1215 — *Magna Charta*

English nobles forced King John to sign the Magna Charta, which gave nobles a share of the power of government.

A.D. 1265 — *Parliament*

English nobles organized a group, called Parliament, to meet with the King and give him their views about how the government should be run.

A.D. 1570 — *Iroquois Confederacy Council*

The tribes of the Iroquois Nation set up a representa tive government, called the Confederacy Council, to make decisions for the entire nation.

A.D. 1689 — *English Bill of Rights*

The English Parliament wrote a Bill of Rights to protect the rights of the people and to put limits on the power of the king and queen.

INSPIRATIONS FOR THE U.S. CONSTITUTION

When Americans decided to set up their own government, they didn't have any precise models or examples to work from—the United States was the first country of its kind in the world. Americans used many ideas, from many sources, in creating their government.

The Ancient World

From the **Code of Hammurabi** came the idea of writing down laws so that citizens could know and understand them. The idea of rule by the people came from the **Direct Democracies** of Ancient Greece. And from Ancient Rome came the idea of **Representative Democracy**, which makes democracy possible when a country has a large population.

England

From the **Magna Charta** and the **English Bill of Rights** came the idea of limiting the power of government to protect the people against tyranny. The **Magna Charta** also provided an example of separating power between different parts of the government. In England, a Parliament was created to share power with the king or queen.

The New World

From the Iroquois came the idea of a confederacy, or partnership, of many groups. Each group was separate, but when there was an event that affected them all, such as a war or a peace treaty, the **Confederacy Council** met to make a decision on the matter. Each group (or for the Iroquois, each tribe) had one vote in the confederacy.

The United States Constitution: established a representative democracy, guaranteed the rights of citizens, and separated power among different branches of government. The United States is made up of states which retain control over local matters.

 UNIT A
SUMMARY

The U.S. government is a little more than 200 years old. It is based on the ideas that

- Laws are written down;
- People share the power of government;
- People elect representatives to run their government;
- If a government is bad, the people have a right to change it;
- Government must be fair to all the people.

These ideas are important to every American today. But these ideas did not start in the United States. These ideas are much older than the U.S. government. These ideas have grown slowly for many centuries.

When the government of the United States began, the people of the United States believed that these ideas were good. They believed that these ideas would guarantee that the people of the United States would be free. So the people who started the U.S. government used these old ideas to form their new government in the New World.

- The idea that laws **should be written down** started in the ancient Middle East. The most important early laws were those of King Hammurabi in ancient Babylon.

- The idea that **people should share the power of government** started in the city states of ancient Greece.

- The idea that **people should elect representatives to run their government** started in ancient Rome. It also existed in the New World among the tribes of the Iroquois Nation.

- The idea that **if a government is bad, the people should have a right to change it** started in England.

- The idea that **government must be fair to all the people** also started in England.

UNIT A QUIZ

*Decide whether each statement below is **true** or **false**. Write **T** or **F** on your own paper. Then write a sentence which tells **why** each false statement is false.*

___ 1. A law is a rule made by a government which people must obey.

___ 2. People need laws so that they will know what they may do, what they may not do, and what they must do.

___ 3. Laws help keep order and prevent confusion.

___ 4. The earliest written set of laws that we know about came from ancient Rome.

___ 5. Laws should be written down so that everyone will be treated the same.

___ 6. Laws should be written down so that everyone will know what the punishment is if they break a law.

___ 7. Government is a way of making decisions.

___ 8. All governments make their decisions in the same way.

___ 9. The form of government in which one person makes all the decisions is called anarchy.

___ 10. A king or queen is called a monarch.

___ 11. Dictators rule as they please and often get their power by force.

___ 12. A democracy is a government in which the people have a say in making the decisions.

___ 13. In all democracies, the people take a direct part in making the decisions and running the government.

___ 14. In a representative democracy, the decisions are made by the king or queen.

___ 15. A republic is another name for a dictatorship.

___ 16. The idea of direct democracy came from ancient Greece.

___ 17. Democracy means rule by the people.

___ 18. Direct democracy works best in places where the population is very large.

___ 19. The idea of representative democracy came from ancient Greece.

___ 20. Most governments in the United States today are representative democracies.

___ 21. The only direct democracies in the United States today are in state governments.

___ 22. The Iroquois Nation was governed by representative councils.

___ 23. The 13 colonies in the New World were settled mostly by people from Greece and Rome.

___ 24. At one time the monarch in England had absolute power.

___ 25. In the early 1200s, King John of England decided that it was best for him to share his power with the nobles in England.

___ 26. The Magna Charta was the first constitution of ancient Rome.

___ 27. The English nobles started the English Parliament because they wanted the king to listen to their opinions.

___ 28. The idea that the people have the right to change a government if it is bad came from England.

___ 29. The English Bill of Rights said that anyone who was accused of a crime had the right to a trial by a jury.

___ 30. The English settlers in the New World wanted to keep all the rights they had gained in England.

Learning Objectives for Unit B

When you have finished this unit, you will be able to:

- Explain what a social contract is and identify the Mayflower Compact.

- Identify the House of Burgesses.

- Explain what a constitution is.

- Identify the Fundamental Orders of Connecticut.

- Explain why people need a written constitution.

- Identify the Declaration of Independence.

- Explain why the 13 colonies decided to break away from Britain.

- Identify the Articles of Confederation.

- Explain the main problem of the Articles of Confederation.

- Explain why the Constitutional Convention wrote a new U.S. Constitution.

- Recognize important people who helped establish the U.S. government.

- Explain the role of compromise in writing the U.S. Constitution.

- Explain what a federal system is.

- Explain what separation of powers means.

- Tell how the state constitutions and the U.S. Constitution are alike.

- Identify the Bill of Rights in the state and U.S. Constitutions.

- Explain why the Bill of Rights was added to the U.S. Constitution.

- Name rights guaranteed by the state constitutions and by the U.S. Constitution.

NEW GOVERNMENTS IN THE NEW WORLD

You have learned that every group of people has some form of government—some system for making rules, enforcing those rules, and carrying on the business of the group.

But when a new group gets together, who decides what form of government the group will have? How does the new government get started?

In this unit, you will learn some of the forms of governments which a group might start. You will also learn what forms of governments the settlers in the New World started.

TOWN HALL OF JAMESTOWN
Jamestown was one of the first settlements in the New World. The community was governed by the House of Burgesses, which held meetings in this building.

CHAPTER 6
How Governments Start

When a new group gets together, the people need rules. They need some system of government.

What form of government will they have?

Governments do not just happen. Someone, or some group of people, must decide what form of government a group will have.

What Would You Do?

Pretend that you are a member of a new group. Your group must set up a government.

- What form of government will you choose?
- How will you decide?

To help with your decision, you might think about the forms of government other groups have had. You learned about some of these in Unit A.

You also might want to think about how well each of these forms of government worked.

- Were the people happy with their form of government?
- What problems did each government have?

You would need a whole course to study how each different form of government works. In this Unit, you will focus on who makes decisions for the group.

Who Has Power?

The first questions you might want to ask about each form of government are: *Who has the power? Who makes the decisions?*

Here are the ways that decisions are made in some forms of government.

One Person Rules

Dictatorship

If one person in the group has a lot more power than anyone else, the form of government might be a **dictatorship**. A dictatorship means that one person has all the power. In a dictatorship, the people do not have any say in running the government.

Monarchy

If the ruler is a member of a family which has ruled for a long time, the government is a **monarchy**. A monarchy means rule by one person who is born into a ruling family. A monarch might be called a king, a queen, an emperor, an empress, a czar, or a czarina. In a powerful monarchy, the people do not have any say in running the government unless the monarch agrees to listen to the people's ideas and advice.

A Few People Rule

If a few people in the group have a lot more power than the other people, the form of government is an **oligarchy**. Oligarchy means *rule by a few*. The few who rule might be the military. In an oligarchy, most of the people do not have any say in running the government.

No One Can Agree on a Form of Government

If several people in the group want power, but they can't agree on how to run things, the group might not have any form of government. This is called **anarchy**.

Anarchy usually doesn't last very long. The people in the group might argue. They might even have a war. Sooner or later one side will win, or two or more small groups will compromise.

 Compromise means that everyone gets part of what they want and gives in a bit to what the others want.

The People Share Power

If the people in the group agree to share power, the form of government is a **democracy**. In a democracy, the people have a say in choosing leaders and making rules. If the people are going to share the power of government, they must get together and make an agreement about just exactly how things will work.

Ideas to Think About

Here are some questions you might think about as you decide what form of government you want.

- Who will make the decisions for the group?

- Will one person make all the decisions?

- Will a small group make all the decisions?

- Will everyone in the group help make the decisions?

- Who will choose the leaders of the group?

- Will the leaders be those with a lot of power?

- Will the leaders be those who have a lot of money?

- Will everyone have an equal chance to be a leader?

- Do you want to help make the decisions for the group?

- Do you want to help choose the leaders?

- Would you like to be a leader yourself?

Think About It

1. Why did you choose the form of government you did?
2. How would you start the new government?

CHAPTER 7

Some Early Governments in the New World

English Settlers in the New World

When English settlers came to the New World, they came in small groups. Each group was responsible for starting its own government. Each group had to decide just what form of government it would have.

The settlers thought about the government they had known in England. They thought about the king and how much power he had. They thought about Parliament and how Parliament had struggled to get a share of power in the government. They thought about how few rights people had when the king had all the power. They thought about the new rights which the people had struggled to get.

The settlers remembered about the governments of the ancient Middle East and the first written laws. They also remembered about the governments of ancient Greece and Rome and the power which the citizens had in their own government. You read about these ancient governments in Unit A.

The settlers met people already living in the New World who controlled their own government. You read about the government of the Iroquois Nation in Unit A.

All of these thoughts helped the settlers decide what form of government they wanted in the New World.

Agreements and Contracts

Leslie Makes a Deal

Leslie's band had a great summer. They played for several dances and entered two contests. They had even started using some of their own songs.

Now a big dance was coming up at school. Leslie and the other girls in the band wanted more than anything to play for that dance. Irene was working on a new song which she was sure everyone at school would like, and Dolores' guitar was better than ever.

But there was one problem. Things at school weren't going so well for Leslie. She was failing math, and she was sure that Mrs. Roper in biology hated her. Nothing ever went right in biology lab, and Leslie's test grades were just on the edge of failing there, too.

The rule at Leslie's school was that only students who were passing everything could be in extracurricular activities. Leslie figured that playing for the school dance was an extracurricular activity. She also figured that with her as leader of the band, the band's chances for getting this job were zero.

The other girls in the band talked it over. They decided they should at least give it a try. No harm in asking, they thought. No one else in the band was failing anything yet this year. Linda's English grades and Dolores' history grades were a bit shaky, but so far both were passing.

Mr. Sylvester was in charge of arrangements for school dances. As teachers went, he wasn't too bad. The girls decided they'd take a chance. They'd go talk to him. What did they have to lose?

Tuesday after school all four girls went to see Mr. Sylvester. Irene did the talking. She made a good case. She told Mr. Sylvester that their band wanted to play for the school dance next month. She didn't even bring up the idea of grades or extracurricular activities.

Mr. Sylvester listened as Irene told him about the band. He said he'd heard about them. His son had gone to a dance where they played last summer. He'd heard they were very good. Leslie began to feel hopeful.

But then Mr. Sylvester asked if the girls knew about the school's extracurricular activity policy. Everyone who is in the school's extracurricular activities must be passing all her classes, he explained.

"I'll check with all your teachers tomorrow," he told the girls. "Then I'll let you know."

Leslie's heart sank. "That's the end of that," she was sure.

When Mrs. Bailey, the principal, sent for Leslie the next day, Leslie guessed it was about her math grades. And she was right. But Mrs. Bailey didn't say what Leslie was expecting.

"I understand your band wants to play for the school dance next month," Mrs. Bailey told Leslie.

"Uh, yes." Leslie prepared herself for the worst.

"I'd like to see you do that, Leslie," Mrs. Bailey said. "But we've got to do something about this passing rule."

Leslie was hoping that "do something about the passing rule" meant they could forget it just this once. But, no, that's not quite what Mrs. Bailey had in mind.

"Mrs. Roper tells me she thinks you can pass biology with a little more work. But I'm really concerned about your math grade."

Leslie couldn't think of anything to say, so she just looked at the floor.

"I'll make a deal with you, Leslie," Mrs. Bailey continued. "Since all the other girls in the band are passing, and since they couldn't play without you, I'll make a special deal with you. Your math teacher has agreed to let you take your last math test over. If you pass that test, you'll have a better chance of passing math this semester.

Just then Mrs. Bailey's secretary came to the door and told her she was needed in the gym. While Mrs. Bailey was gone, Leslie thought about the deal that Mrs. Bailey had offered her. Mrs. Bailey was trying to be fair, she decided.

Leslie believed she could handle biology. But math. She didn't even want to think about math. Passing that math test would not be easy. Leslie hated math. If she passed, she'd have to work awfully hard. That would mean a lot less time with her boyfriend and with the band. It was so much nicer to spend her time going out, or learning new songs, or playing with the band.

But passing the math test was part of Mrs. Bailey's deal. And Leslie didn't see any way around it.

Leslie thought about it a long time before she made up her mind. A deal was like a contract, and Leslie knew about contracts. Every time the band played for pay they made a contract.

Mrs. Bailey's contract was not about money. But a contract was a contract, and when you made a contract, you had to stick to whatever you agreed to.

The terms of Mrs. Bailey's contract were very simple. She was giving Leslie a chance to play with her band at the school dance. All Leslie had to do in return was work extra hard on math. Leslie decided it was worth it.

When Mrs. Bailey returned, Leslie was smiling. "It's a deal," she said. And somehow she knew she would do it.

Social Contracts

Deals or contracts are agreements among people. Each person in a contract promises to do something or give something. Each person also expects to get something from the contract.

When Leslie's band played for pay, they made a contract. The band gave work and got money. The place where they played gave money and got music.

All contracts do not involve money. Leslie's contract with her principal did not involve money. In this contract, Leslie gave some time and work to pass math. She got a chance to play at the school dance.

When people make an agreement with each other about how rules will be made, they are making a contract. This kind of contract is called a **social contract**. The people involved in a social contract give

something and expect to get something. The people agree to give some power to their leaders. In return, the people get whatever benefits they and their leaders have agreed on.

An important thing to remember about a contract is that it is an agreement between two sides. Both sides agree to something. If one side doesn't keep its promise, the other side is not bound to its agreement.

If Leslie's band had a contract to play in a club for money and the band didn't show up, the club wouldn't owe the band any money.

In Leslie's contract with Mrs. Bailey, if Leslie didn't make passing grades in math and biology, Mrs. Bailey wouldn't have to let Leslie play at the school dance.

If people make a social contract with certain leaders and those leaders do not follow their agreement with the people, the people can choose new leaders.

The Mayflower Compact

In the year 1620, 102 people sailed to America on a ship named *Mayflower*. They sailed 66 days across the Atlantic Ocean. They planned to start a new life in the New World where they could be free to have their own kind of church.

The people were English. King James of England was their king. But their new home was far from England. They would need rules of their own for everyday life.

While they were still on the ship, the people talked about how they would make rules in their new home. One group wanted to make all the rules. The rest of the people didn't like that idea. They threatened to leave.

Finally the people decided to make a contract among themselves. They decided that everyone in the group would help make the group's rules and choose the group's leaders. They didn't want just one person to have all the power in their new government. They didn't want just a few people to have power in their new government. They all wanted to have a share of the power in their new government.

The people on the *Mayflower* wrote down their agreement on paper. Each of the 41 adult men signed his name. Each promised to obey the rules the group would make.

Today we call the people on the *Mayflower* "the Pilgrims." The Pilgrims made a **social contract** with each other. They named their contract after their ship. They called their contract the **Mayflower Compact.**

The Pilgrims settled in Plymouth in what is now the state of Massachusetts. The **social contract** they made while they were still on the *Mayflower* became the basis for their government. This contract started a **direct democracy.**

What did the people give when they made their social contract?

- Each person gave a promise to stay with the group and obey the rules.
- Each person gave a promise to work to make their new life successful.

What did the people get when they made their social contract?

- Each person got the right to help make the rules for the group.
- Each person got the security of a group working together.

The **Mayflower Compact** was a **social contract.**

It started **direct democracy** in the New World.

Think About It

1. What is a contract?
2. What is a social contract?
3. Name the social contract signed by the people on the *Mayflower*.
4. Why was it important for the people to agree to this social contract?
5. Why do you think these settlers wanted to start a democracy in their new home?

Representative Democracy in the New World

Not all of the settlements in the New World were small enough for direct democracies.

Most of the colonies had **representative democracies.**

The first **representative democracy** in the English colonies was in Jamestown, Virginia. It was started in 1619, one year before the Mayflower landed in Plymouth, Massachusetts.

The House of Burgesses

The representative government in Jamestown was called the **House of Burgesses.**

Members of the House of Burgesses were elected by the adult men of Jamestown to represent all the people of

Jamestown. Members of the House of Burgesses made laws for Jamestown.

Jamestown was too large to have a direct democracy. So the men elected certain individuals to represent them. In this way, they all had some voice in the way their government was run.

An old English word for a town is *burg*. You may have heard of Williamsburg or Pittsburg. These mean the same as Williamstown or Pittstown. They are towns named after people named William or Pitt.

The House of Burgesses meant a group or assembly of citizens from the burg or town. It is the same as saying the *House of Townspeople*.

Think About It

1. How was the government of Jamestown, Virginia, different from the government of Plymouth, Massachusetts?
2. What was the name of the governing assembly in the first representative democracy in the New World?
3. Does your town have a representative democracy or a direct democracy?

The First Constitution in the New World

Not all groups of settlers in the New World had democracies.

The Puritans of Massachusetts Bay did not have a democracy.

Among the Puritans, the ministers were the leaders of the people. These leaders made the rules. The people were told to obey. The people did not have the right to help make the rules.

If the people did not like the rules, they could not change them.

If the people were not happy with the leaders, they did not have the right to choose new leaders.

Some of the Puritans became very unhappy with their leaders. They believed the leaders were unfair. The people wanted a part in making their own rules.

Small groups of Puritans left the Massachusetts Bay colony in 1635 and 1636. They moved to new areas so they could set up new governments.

Some of these groups moved to what is now the state of Connecticut. One of their leaders was **Thomas Hooker**. Thomas Hooker wanted to start a democratic government in his new settlement.

After these settlers had lived in Connecticut a few years, they decided to write a **constitution.**

*A **constitution** says who will choose the leaders, who will make the laws, who will carry out the laws, and how laws will be changed.*

The Fundamental Orders of Connecticut

In 1639 the settlers in Connecticut wrote a **constitution**. They called their constitution **The Fundamental Orders of Connecticut.**

The Fundamental Orders of Connecticut gave the people a say in how the government was run. Because their rules were written down in a **constitution**, the people's rights and freedoms were protected. No leader could make rules which threatened the people's rights.

This constitution said:

- The people will have a **representative democracy.**
- The voters will elect representatives from each town to be members of a **representative assembly.**
- The voters will elect the officers of the representative assembly.
- The voters will elect a governor for Connecticut.
- The voters will elect judges.

The **Fundamental Orders of Connecticut** was the first written constitution among the English settlers in the New World. It told how the government of one colony would be run.

Later, other colonies followed the example of the Connecticut settlers and wrote constitutions for their own governments.

This first constitution was a **social contract**. In this contract the people gave certain powers to their representatives. The people got an orderly government with the right to help choose the leaders for their group.

Think About It

1. How was the government of the Massachusetts Bay colony different from the government in Jamestown, Virginia, or Plymouth, Massachusetts?
2. What is a **constitution?**
3. What was the name of the first constitution in the New World?
4. Who was Thomas Hooker?
5. Why did Thomas Hooker leave the Massachusetts Bay Colony?
6. If you had been a Puritan in 1636, would you have stayed in the Massachusetts Bay Colony? Or would you have gone to Connecticut with Thomas Hooker? Why would you have made this choice?
7. If you had helped write the Fundamental Orders of Connecticut, would you have made any changes in what this constitution said? Why or why not?
8. If you would have made changes in the Fundamental Orders of Connecticut, what would they have been?

THOMAS HOOKER

My name is Thomas Hooker. I am a Puritan minister. But I am different from most of the other Puritan ministers.

Most Puritan ministers believe that the minister alone must be the leader of the people. They believe that the minister has the right to make all the rules. They do not let the people help make the rules. They do not listen to the people if the people disagree with the leaders.

I believe that these ministers are wrong. I believe that the people should share in making the rules. I believe that the people should choose their own leaders.

Later, if the people are unhappy with a leader, the people have a right to choose another leader. The leaders should always listen to what the people think.

Along with other unsatisfied Puritans, Thomas Hooker left the Massachusetts Bay settlement to start a new, more democratic settlement called Connecticut.

The Road to Independence

The Colonists Become "Americans"

As the years went by, more settlers came to the New World. More colonies were started. More new governments were formed.

All the colonies were technically under the rule of the British king and the British Parliament. Some of the colonies had governors appointed by Parliament.

However, the colonies were far away from Britain. The king and Parliament didn't have much to do with the day-to-day business of government in the colonies. The people in each colony mostly took care of day-to-day things themselves.

More and more the colonists stopped thinking of themselves as English people or British people. They were Americans.

Trouble with Britain

In 1707 England, Wales, and Scotland joined together to form **Great Britain**. The King of England now became the King of Great Britain.

From now on we will talk about **Britain** rather than England.

Britain Goes to War

In 1754 Britain got into a war with France. This war started over a disagreement between Britain and France about who owned the land in western Pennsylvania and Ohio. The war went on for nine years.

During this war, the British king and Parliament started to take more control of what went on in the colonies.

For 150 years the colonies had been taking more and more control of their own affairs. Now most of the colonists were not a bit happy that the British government wanted to tell them what to do.

In the years after the war, Parliament passed several laws which the colonists thought were unfair.

- Parliament made rules about where new settlements could be made in America.
- Parliament let the British governors in the colonies send a colonist to Britain for trial.
- When Boston protested the laws, Parliament passed a law closing the Boston Harbor.

The Declaration of Independence

In Congress, July 4, 1776, the unanimous Declaration of the
thirteen united States of America

When in the Course of human events, it becomes necessary for one people to dissolve the political bands which have connected them with another, and to assume among the Powers of the earth, the separate and equal station to which the Laws of Nature and of Nature's God entitle them, a decent respect to the opinions of mankind requires that they should declare the causes which impel them to the separation.

We hold these truths to be self-evident, that all men are created equal, that they are endowed by their Creator with certain unalienable Rights, that among these are Life, Liberty and the pursuit of Happiness. That to secure these rights, Governments are instituted among Men, deriving their just powers from the consent of the governed. That whenever any Form of Government becomes destructive of these ends, it is the Right of the People to alter or to abolish it, and to institute new Government, laying its foundation on such principles and organizing its powers in such form, as to them shall seem most likely to effect their Safety and Happiness. Prudence, indeed, will dictate that Governments long established should not be changed for light and transient causes; and accordingly all experience hath shown, that mankind are more disposed to suffer, while evils are sufferable, than to right themselves by abolishing the forms to which they are accustomed. But when a long train of abuses and usurpations, pursing invariably the same Object evinces a design to reduce them under absolute Despotism, it is their right, it is their duty, to throw off such Government, and to provide new Guards for their future security.—Such has been the patient sufferance of these Colonies; and such is now the necessity which constrains them to alter their former Systems of Government. The history of the present King of Great Britain is a history of repeated injuries and usurpations, all having in direct object the establishment of an absolute Tyranny over these States. To prove this, let Facts be submitted to a candid world.

[A list of wrongs done to the colonies by the King of England and the British Government follows.]

We, therefore, the Representatives of the united States of America, in General Congress, Assembled, appealing to the Supreme Judge of the world for the rectitude of our intentions, do, in the Name, and by Authority of the good People of these Colonies, solemnly publish and declare, That these United Colonies are, and of Right ought to be Free and Independent States; that they are Absolved from all Allegiance to the British Crown, and that all political connection between them and the State of Great Britain, is and ought to be totally dissolved; and that as Free and Independent States, they have full Power to levy War, conclude Peace, contract Alliances, establish Commerce, and to do all other Acts and Things which Independent States may of right do. And for the support of this Declaration, with a firm reliance on the Protection of Divine Providence, we mutually pledge to each other our Lives, our Fortunes and our sacred Honor.

Taxation Without Representation

Another big problem had to do with money.

The long war left Britain with a very large war debt. The king and Parliament decided that the colonists should help pay this debt. So Parliament passed new tax laws.

The colonists now had to pay taxes on sugar, molasses, tea, and many other items they bought from other countries. The colonists also had to pay a tax on all printed papers—even on their newspapers.

"What right does Parliament have to tax us?" the colonists wanted to know. *"We don't have representatives in Parliament. They didn't ask our opinion. We didn't vote on these new tax laws."*

*"This is **taxation without representation**, and we don't like it."*

Long ago, before Parliament had gained a share of power in England, the king taxed the nobles without asking their advice. This had made the nobles angry. In fact, this was the main reason the nobles started Parliament in the first place.

Now Parliament was treating the colonists the same way the king had treated the nobles in England long ago. The colonists didn't like this at all.

Parliament's Opinion

Parliament thought they had a right to pass these new laws. After all, the colonies belonged to Britain.

Parliament believed the colonists should be happy to do whatever Parliament said was good for Britain.

The Colonists' Opinion

The new laws Parliament passed made the colonists very angry. The colonists had been handling their own affairs for many years. Now Parliament was butting in.

Parliament might know what was best for Britain, but the colonists themselves knew what was best for the colonies.

The colonists definitely did not believe that Parliament's new laws were best for the colonies.

Think About It

1. Why were the colonists angry with Parliament?
2. What does taxation without representation mean?
3. If you had been a colonist, what would you have advised the colonies to do about their problems with Britain?

The Colonists Decide to Act

In 1774 all but one of the colonies sent representatives to a meeting in Philadelphia. This meeting was called the **First Continental Congress.**

The representatives wrote a **Declaration of Rights** to send to the king in Britain. They hoped the king would listen to their advice and stop the unfair laws which Parliament was making. But the king paid no attention to the Declaration of Rights.

Plans for Independence

The next year (1775), representatives from all 13 colonies came to Philadelphia for the **Second Continental Congress**. By now war had started between the British soldiers and the colonists. The Second Continental Congress organized a Continental Army and put George Washington in charge. Then they asked Thomas Jefferson to write a paper saying why the colonists were fighting Britain and why they wanted to be free and independent of Britain.

*"Why should we keep being colonies of Britain?" the colonists thought, "We know what is best for us. But the king and Parliament will not listen to us. We should break our ties with Britain. We should be **independent**."*

The paper which Thomas Jefferson wrote was called the **Declaration of Independence**. It said that the 13 British colonies would not be colonies anymore. From now on they would be free and independent states.

The colonists wanted to be sure the rest of the world understood why they were breaking away from Britain. They wanted the rest of the world to be friendly to them when they became independent states.

The members of the **Second Continental Congress** approved the **Declaration of Independence** on **July 4, 1776.**

That is why we celebrate the 4th of July. July 4 is our nation's birthday.

Thomas Jefferson

My name is Thomas Jefferson. I am a landowner and planter in Virginia. I have been a member of the House of Burgesses and am now a delegate to the Second Continental Congress.

My fellow delegates asked me to write a paper to declare to the world that the colonies are independent from Britain.

I have read ideas about government written by European thinkers. I have thought about what form of government is best for the people. I believe government should be based on agreement among the people—a *social contract*. People have the right to change their government if it is bad.

I believe that government should always be based on free and open discussions.

Government should follow the will of the majority. It should also always protect the rights of the minority.

45

The Declaration of Independence

The most important idea in the Declaration of Independence is that a government should only exist if the people agree to it.

A fair government must rest on the consent of the people.

The **Declaration of Independence** has three sections:

- **Section 1** lists rights that all people should have.
- **Section 2** tells what Britain has done wrong.
- **Section 3** says the colonies are breaking off to be free and independent.

Blaming the King

Section 2 of the Declaration of Independence gives a long list of what Britain has done which made the colonists angry. It blames the king for all these wrongs. Actually, it was Parliament which passed the laws the colonists didn't like. But since the king was the head of the government, the Declaration of Independence was directed at him.

Think About It

1. What did the representatives at the First Continental Congress hope to accomplish?
2. Why was a Second Continental Congress needed?
3. What action did the representatives at the Second Continental Congress take? What were their reasons?
4. Why did the Declaration of Independence blame the British king for the wrongs that angered the colonists?

What Does the Declaration of Independence Say?

Section 1: Rights of the People

When one group of people decides they must break off from another group which they have been a part of, they should give the reasons for this decision.

We believe the following ideas are so true that anyone can understand them:

- All men are created equal.
- The Creator gave all men some rights that no one should take away. **These are the right to life, the right to freedom, and the right to seek happiness.**

People form governments so they can protect these important rights.

The only fair and just powers a government has are the ones its people give it.

If a government doesn't protect the rights of its people, the people should either change the government or replace it with a new government which does protect their rights.

People should not change their governments for no reason. But when a government keeps on treating its people unfairly over and over, the people have a right and a duty to put an end to the bad government and form a better government.

This is exactly what the 13 colonies have decided to do.

Section 2: What Britain Has Done Wrong

The king has a long record of unfair acts. We will tell you what they are:

- He will not agree to the good laws we make for ourselves.
- He will not let our governors pass laws which are good for the colonies.
- He has tried to stop our own lawmakers from running our government.
- He has tried to control our judges.
- He has kept armies which we didn't want or need in the colonies during peacetime.
- He has tried to use his army to control our own local governments.
- He has tried to make his law overrule the laws we make for ourselves.
- He has made us keep large numbers of soldiers in our homes.
- He has let his soldiers murder our people and not be punished.
- He has cut off our trade with the rest of the world.
- He has made us pay taxes that we didn't agree to.
- He has denied us the right of trial by jury.
- He has made us go to Britain to be tried for crimes we did not do.

- He has taken away our best laws that protect our freedoms.
- He has taken away the lawmakers we elected and let his Parliament make our laws.
- He is making war on us, killing our people, and destroying our cities.

Section 3: Why the Colonies Are Breaking Off from Britain

We, the colonists, **have** kept **on asking the king t**o treat us fairly. He keeps on refusing. He is a tyrant and not fit to rule.

■ A tyrant is a cruel, unfair ruler.

We have also talked to Parliament and the British people. We have asked them to treat us fairly. They, too, have refused.

So we are now telling all the world that we are not colonies of Britain anymore. From now on we are free and independent states. And we all promise to help each other stay free.

Who Are "All Men"?

You will remember that in Ancient Greece and Ancient Rome all the citizens could have a part in running the government. But the citizens did not include all the people.

This was also true in the 13 colonies and the early United States. When Thomas Jefferson wrote "all men are created equal" in the Declaration of Independence, he really meant "all white, adult males." When the Declaration of Independence was signed, women were not allowed to take part in government the same as men. Most black people living in the 13 colonies were slaves. They had no rights as citizens. The Native Americans (Indians) living in the 13 colonies had no rights, either.

As the years have gone by, women, blacks, and Native Americans have gained all the rights of citizenship. Even young people have been given more rights. **These groups didn't start out with the same rights as white men. They had to work hard to get their rights.**

The Declaration of Independence was a beginning. It started a system of government in which all the people could be free, even if it didn't give full rights of citizenship to all the people who lived in the 13 new states right from the start.

Think About It

1. Who wrote the Declaration of Independence?
2. Tell what each section of the Declaration of Independence is about.
3. What group of people did the Declaration of Independence mean when it said "all men are created equal"? What groups did it leave out?
4. Why is the Declaration of Independence such an important document?

New Government for the New States

13 New Constitutions

After the Declaration of Independence was signed, each new state began to write a constitution for its new government. The constitutions of the 13 new states were not exactly alike. However, they all shared some major ideas.

Each state wanted to:

- give its people the right to have a say in how their government was run.
- give its people the right to elect their own lawmakers and other government leaders.
- guarantee its people all the rights of free people.
- protect the rights of its people by writing down the laws in a **constitution** so that everyone would know what the laws were and everyone would be treated the same.

Remember: a **constitution** is a plan for government.

What Did These New Constitutions Say?

Representative Democracy

Each state's constitution set up a representative democracy. The voters in each state elected representatives to make the decisions of government for all the people.

Separation of Powers

Each state's constitution separated the powers of government. The powers were divided among three branches.

- **Legislative branch**. This branch makes the laws.
- **Executive branch.** This branch enforces the laws.
- **Judicial branch.** This branch decides if the laws are fair. It also decides if the laws have been broken and settles problems which have to do with the laws.

Each state's constitution divided its government into these three branches so that no one part of the government would have too much power.

The states wanted to be sure that they had **governments of laws, not of individuals**.

- No person would be above the law.
- No matter who the leaders were at any one time, the constitutions told what everyone could do.
- The constitutions made sure that everyone would be treated the same.

Bill of Rights

Each state's constitution also had a Bill of Rights—a list of all the rights of free people. The Bill of Rights guaranteed that the government would not take these rights away.

Each state's Bill of Rights gave its people the right to

- say what they wanted to say and even print their opinions in the newspaper;
- get together in groups when they wanted to;
- practice their own religion;
- have a say about how much tax they paid;
- have a fair trial by a jury;
- be safe from cruel and unusual punishment; and
- be safe from unlawful search of their homes.

A Social Contract

Each state's constitution was a social contract. The people gave something and got something.

- The people gave their state govern ment the power to make laws, en force those laws, settle disputes, and carry on the day-to-day affairs of the government.
- The people got order and security and a guarantee that their freedoms and rights would not be taken away.

Think About It

1. What form of government did the state constitutions set up?
2. Why did the state constitutions divide their governments into 3 branches?
3. Why did the states want a government of laws, not of individuals?
4. Name 4 rights which each state's Bill of Rights guaranteed to the people.
5. Why was it so important that each state's constitution contain a Bill of Rights?

CHAPTER 11

13 Separate Governments Get Together

When the Declaration of Independence was signed, the 13 colonies became 13 separate states.

All of the 13 new states were at war with Britain. They knew that they had to work together to win the war.

Representatives from the new states met at the **Second Continental Congress**. They talked about the problems of all the states. The members of the Second Continental Congress realized that they had to work together to solve their problems. They believed that the 13 states should form one united government.

The same group which had written the Declaration of Independence now wrote a plan which would join all 13 states into one national government. This plan was called the **Articles of Confederation**. It was the **first national constitution** of the new states.

The Articles of Confederation

The Articles of Confederation created a new nation—the United States of America. The Articles of Confederation started the first central government for the 13 states. The Articles of Confederation gave the people of all 13 states a sense of unity and cooperation.

However, the Articles of Confederation did not give the national government much power. Each state wanted to have control of its own affairs, so the Articles of Confederation created a very weak central government. In fact, the central government had so little power that it was almost helpless.

What Did the Articles of Confederation Say?

The Articles of Confederation created a national **Congress.**

Each state sent representatives to this Congress, but each state had only one vote in Congress, no matter how large or small its population was.

The Congress could make laws, but it had no power to enforce these laws.

The Congress could not control trade among the states or trade with other countries.

The Congress could not even collect taxes from the states. This was a very big problem because the United States still had a very large war debt from its war for independence from Britain. Some of the states refused to pay their share of this debt.

A Social Contract

The Articles of Confederation were a **social contract.**

When the 13 states signed the Articles of Confederation, they **gave** something and **got** something.

The states **gave** the central government a very small amount of power.

The states **got** a sense of unity and a weak central government. They did not get a government which could solve their problems.

When the states made this social contract, they did not give enough. As a result, they did not get what they really wanted or needed.

The Articles of Confederation got a national government started. This first national constitution gave the states a feeling of unity. But how long could the government it created last?

The problems of the new national government were getting bigger, but the government was too weak to do anything about these problems. Some people were afraid that either anarchy or tyranny would result.

The Constitutional Convention

The people of the 13 states believed that they had come too far to let anarchy or tyranny threaten their new government.

They were happy with the freedoms they had in their own states. But they realized that there were some problems which only a central government could handle. Unless they all worked together in a central government, these new independent states might not survive.

THE CONSTITUTIONAL CONVENTION
One of the greatest gatherings of political thinkers and statesmen ever. George Washington, the president of the Convention, is standing behind the desk (at center).

The states liked the idea of a central government which the Articles of Confederation had started. But they realized that some improvements needed to be made before this central government could do its job well.

In 1787, 11 years after the Declaration of Independence was signed, the states sent representatives to a **Constitutional Convention** in Philadelphia. At first these representatives tried to revise the Articles of Confederation. They hoped that if they made a few improvements, the central government would work better.

The representatives soon realized that the weak central government which the Articles of Confederation had created simply could not handle the growing problems of the United States.

A completely new constitution was needed.

The members of this Constitutional Convention worked for three and a half months. They talked and they argued. Sometimes their disagreements were very heated. But they all agreed on one thing: they wanted a national government which was strong enough to keep the United States free.

Members of the Constitutional Convention

Who were the people at the Constitutional Convention?

There were 55 delegates to the Constitutional Convention. All of the delegates were white men. They were all community leaders who were rich enough to spend several months away from home at a convention. Many of the delegates had been a part of the nation's struggle for independence.

George Washington presided over the Constitutional Convention. George Washington became the first President of the United States. Benjamin Franklin, age 81, was the oldest delegate. James Madison, a delegate from Virginia, later became the fourth President of the United States. He kept a journal of the meetings.

Think About It

1. Why did the states decide to join together into the United States?
2. What was the name of the first plan for a central government of the United States?
3. Why didn't the Articles of Confederation work?

A New Constitution

A Federal Government

The members of the Constitutional Convention wrote a new **constitution**—a new plan of government for the United States. This new constitution created a **federal** form of government.

A **federal** government means that a group of states join together to make a national government.

In a federal system:

- all the states are equal;
- all the states keep some power;
- the states give up some of their power to the national government; and
- each state sends representatives to the national government.

Since the states all send representatives to the national government, they are really sharing this power among themselves.

Limited Government

"Ours is a government of law, not of men."—*John Adams, second President of the United States*

The new Constitution gave government certain powers. It also put limits on the power of government. The Constitution lists certain things which the government cannot do. These constitutional limits on government protect the basic human rights of people in the United States.

Similarities to State Governments

The new U.S. Constitution was very much like the state constitutions.

- First, it created a **representative democracy**, just as all the states had.

- Second, the U.S. Constitution divided the federal government into **three branches**—just as the states had. These three branches of government were the same as those in state governments: **legislative, executive, judicial**. Just as in the states, the writers of the U.S. Constitution did not want any one branch of government to get too much power.

- Third, the U.S. Constitution created a **government of law, not of individuals**. No person would be above the law.

The States Disagree

Not all of the decisions about the new Constitution were as easy as deciding on a representative democracy with three branches of government. One big problem was how to organize the legislative branch.

Under the Articles of Confederation, each state had one vote in Congress. All the states had equal lawmaking power.

Some of the states and also some of the writers of the Constitution didn't think this arrangement was fair.

Some of the 13 states were large. They had many people. Others were small. They had fewer people. The people in the large states wanted each person in their state to have as much power in the government as each person in the small states had. The small states wanted to be sure that they had as much power as the large states had.

The writers of the Constitution had a hard job. They needed a plan which

- kept all the states equal with each other and also
- gave all the people in the large states their fair share of representation in the national government.

What the Small States Wanted

The small states wanted every state to have equal power in the central government.

They wanted each state to have one vote in the Congress. This was the same as it had been under the Articles of Confederation.

What the Large States Wanted

The large states disagreed. Each person should be equal, not each state.

If the small number of people in a small state had as much power as the large number of people in a large state, the people in the large state wouldn't have their fair share of power.

The States Compromise

The writers of the Constitution **compromised**. They took some ideas from the small states and some ideas from the large states. Finally, they all agreed.

This is what they decided.

- **Instead of one Congress, they would have a legislature (lawmaking body) with two parts, or "houses."**

- **One house of the legislature would be based on population.**

  Each representative in this house would represent the same number of people, no matter what state the representative was from. So large states would have more representatives than small ones. This made the large states happy. This house would be called the **House of Representatives**. It would be the largest (have the most members) of the two houses of the legislature.

- **The other house of the legislature would have two members from every state, regardless of the state's population.**

  This gave the small states and the large states the same number of representatives in one house of the legislature. This house would be called the **Senate**.

- **Together, both houses of the legislature would be called Congress.**

This compromise made both the small states and the large states happy. Each group got part of what they wanted. Each group gave something to the other side.

The writers of the Constitution made several compromises before they finished their job. No one state got everything it wanted. In the end, the writers felt that the new Constitution would be good for the nation as a whole.

You will learn what the U.S. Constitution says in Unit C.

The Bill of Rights

Before the Constitution could go into effect, nine of the 13 states had to **ratify** (approve) it.

People in the 13 states disagreed about whether the new Constitution should be **ratified** or not.

Some people said, *"Yes. We need a strong central government. Look at the trouble we had with the Articles of Confederation. The Articles gave us a weak central government that could not solve our problems. Without a strong central government, the 13 states will simply fight and argue. We can't come to decisions. We need a central government to keep things orderly and avoid confusion. We need to have some uniformity among the states. And without a strong central government, who would speak for our nation abroad?"*

But other people said, *"No. If we give so much power to a central government, we will surely lose all our freedoms. How can we keep the central government from taking away all the freedoms and rights we won in the Revolution?"*

So, what did the people do?

They compromised. Supporters of the new Constitution promised to write a Bill of Rights as soon as the new Congress met.

The rights in the federal Bill of Rights would be similar to the ones included in each state constitution's Bill of Rights.

The federal Bill of Rights would clearly say what freedoms the people of the United States had. It would guarantee that the central government would never take these rights away.

With the promise of a Bill of Rights, more people supported the Constitution, and finally all 13 states approved it.

A Social Contract

When the 13 states approved the new Constitution, they were making a social contract. They were giving something, and they were getting something.

The states were giving the central government the power to make laws and collect taxes. The states were getting unity and cooperation and strength which would help keep them all free.

Think About It

1. How is the U.S. Constitution different from the Articles of Confederation?
2. What does **federal** mean?
3. How did the Constitutional Convention settle the disagreement between the large and small states?
4. How is the U.S. Constitution like the state constitutions?
5. Why was a Bill of Rights added to the U.S. Constitution?
6. Name two delegates to the Constitutional Convention.

UNIT B SUMMARY

More than 250 years had passed since the Mayflower Compact, the first **social contract** in the New World, was signed. Some direct democracies had been formed in the New World. Many small representative governments had been formed. The population of the New World had grown.

Now 13 separate states had representative governments. Together these 13 states had formed a union—a national representative government called the United States of America.

Each of the new states had a constitution. These constitutions were written down so that all the people could know what the laws were.

These constitutions gave the people freedoms and rights. They let the people have a say in their government. The constitutions even allowed the people to make changes in their laws if the people felt the laws were unfair.

The United States also had a new Constitution. Just as the states' constitutions, the U.S. Constitution was written down. It gave the people freedoms and rights. It let the people have a say in their government.

The U.S. Constitution protected all the people in all the states.

Time Line for Unit B

— 1607 *Jamestown*

The first permanent settlement of English people in North America was set up in Jamestown, Virginia.

— 1619 *House of Burgesses*

The first representative democracy in the English colonies, called the House of Burgesses, was started in Jamestown.

— 1620 *Mayflower Compact*

The adult male Pilgrims on the ship, *Mayflower*, signed a social contract, called the Mayflower Compact, setting up a direct democracy for their new colony.

— 1639 *Fundamental Orders of Connecticut*

The first written constitution in the English colonies, called the Fundamental Orders of Connecticut, was written by settlers in Connecticut.

— 1774 *First Continental Congress*

Representatives of 12 of the American met in Philadelphia and wrote a Declaration of Rights to tell the British king that they were angry about new laws passed by Parliament.

— 1775 *Second Continental Congress*

Representatives from all 13 colonies met in Philadelphia and organized a Continental Army led by George Washington.

— 1776 *Declaration of Independence*

Members of the Second Continental Congress signed the Declaration of Independence, breaking off to be free and independent from Britain. The 13 colonies thus became the 13 new states.

— 1781 **_Articles of Confederation_**

Members of the Second Continental Congress wrote the Articles of Confederation to join all 13 new states into a new nation.

— 1787 **_Constitutional Convention_**

Representatives from the states met in Philadelphia to revise the Articles of Confederation. Instead of revising the Articles, however, they replaced them with a new Constitution.

— 1788 **_U.S. Constitution_**

The U.S. Constitution was ratified (approved) and went into effect.

— 1791 **_Bill of Rights_**

Amendments 1-10, known as the Bill of Rights, were added to the U.S. Constitution.

UNIT B QUIZ

*Decide whether each statement below is **true** or **false**. Write **T** or **F** on your own paper. Then write a sentence which tells **why** each false statement is false.*

___ 1. A dictatorship is a system of government in which one person has all the power.

___ 2. In a monarchy, the king or queen must listen to the people's ideas and advice.

___ 3. In an oligarchy, most of the people do not have any say in running the government.

___ 4. Compromise means that everyone gets part of what they want.

___ 5. Democracy means that several groups want power and can't agree on how to run things.

___ 6. English settlers in the New World wanted a monarchy in which the king had all the power because this had worked well in England.

___ 7. The Mayflower Compact was a social contract which started direct democracy in the New World.

___ 8. A social contract is an agreement among people about how the rules for their group will be made.

___ 9. The first representative democracy in the English colonies was started at Plymouth.

___10. The House of Burgesses in Jamestown was a representative assembly elected by the men of Jamestown.

___11. All of the English settlements in the New World had democratic forms of government.

___12. A constitution is a plan which tells how a government will work.

___13. The Fundamental Orders of Connecticut was the first written constitution among the English settlers in the New World.

___14. The Fundamental Orders of Connecticut provided for a direct democracy.

___15. Thomas Hooker was a Puritan minister who believed that ministers should make all the laws.

___16. The English colonists decided to become independent from Britain because the British King declared war on the colonies.

___17. The most important idea in the Declaration of Independence is that a government should only exist if the people agree to it.

___18. In the Declaration of Independence, all men referred to both men and women.

___19. When the 13 colonies broke away from Britain, they each wrote a constitution.

___20. Separation of powers means that the duties of government are divided among more than one branch of government.

___21. The new states wanted to have governments of laws, not of individuals.

___22. The rights of free people in each state were provided for in a Bill of Rights in each state's constitution.

___23. The Articles of Confederation created a strong central government.

___24. The purpose of the Constitutional Convention of 1787 was to declare independence from Britain.

___25. George Washington, the president of the Constitutional Convention became the first President of the United States.

___26. A federal government is a group of equal states joined together to form a nation.

___27. The U.S. Constitution created a direct democracy just as each state had.

___28. The large states wanted each state to have equal power in the new federal government.

___29. At the Constitutional Convention, the large and small states compromised by creating a Congress with two houses.

___30. A Bill of Rights was added to the U.S. Constitution in order to protect the rights of all the people.

Learning Objectives for Unit C

When you have finished this unit, you will be able to:

- Explain why the U.S. Constitution was written.

- Tell how the U.S. Constitution protects each of the states.

- Tell why the Bill of Rights was added to the U.S. Constitution.

- Tell what three branches of government the U.S. Constitution created.

- Name the rights guaranteed to the people of the United States.

- Tell what amendments give rights to more people in the United States.

- Tell what groups of people are guaranteed the right to vote by the U.S. Constitution.

THE U.S. CONSTITUTION

The United States Constitution was written more than 200 years ago. It is not very long—only about 7,000 words. But these 7,000 words have helped keep the United States together and free for a long time.

In this unit you will learn what the U.S. Constitution says.

Some of the language of the Constitution is hard to understand. Therefore, this Unit uses more modern language.

THE U.S. CONSTITUTION
The original draft of the Constitution is displayed in the National Archives in Washington, D.C.

What Does the U.S. Constitution Say?

The Preamble

The first paragraph of the U.S. Constitution is called the **Preamble** to the Constitution. **Preamble** means introduction.

The **Preamble** of the U.S. Constitution tells six reasons why the Constitution was written:

- **to form a more perfect union**—to set up a central government which would work better than the first one did.
- **to establish justice**—to be sure that all the people in the United States are treated fairly.
- **to insure domestic tranquility**—to keep all 13 states getting along peacefully together.
- **to provide for the common defense**—to protect the whole country against any attacks.
- **to promote the general welfare**—to work for the good of the country as a whole, not just one part of the country.
- **to secure the blessings of liberty to ourselves and our posterity**—to protect the rights of free people now and for future generations.

For many years, students have memorized the Preamble to the U.S. Constitution.

The whole Preamble is printed here for you. Maybe you, also, would like to memorize it.

PREAMBLE
TO THE
UNITED STATES CONSTITUTION

WE, THE PEOPLE of the United States, in order to form a more perfect union, establish justice, insure domestic tranquility, provide for the common defense, promote the general welfare, and secure the blessings of liberty to ourselves and our posterity, do ordain and establish this constitution for the United States of America.

The U.S. Constitution— Seven Articles

The main part of the U.S. Constitution is divided into seven parts called **articles.**

Article 1

Article 1 creates the **legislative branch** of the federal government—the **Congress**. Congress makes laws for the United States.

(Unit D in this book covers the legislative branch.)

Article 2

Article 2 creates the **executive branch** of the federal government. The **President** of the United States is head of the executive branch. The executive branch carries out the laws and runs the day-to-day business of the federal government.

(Unit E covers the executive branch.)

Article 3

Article 3 creates the **judicial branch** of the federal government. The Constitution creates a **Supreme Court** and lets Congress set up lower courts. The judicial branch settles questions about what the laws mean. It also decides when a person has broken a law and what the punishment should be.

(Unit F covers the judicial branch.)

Article 4

Article 4 talks about the relation of the states to each other. It says:

- Each state must honor the laws, records, and legal decisions of all the other states.
- Each state must treat the citizens of all the other states fairly.
- If a person accused of a crime runs away to another state, that person must be returned to the state where the crime was done.
- If a slave runs away to another state, the slave must be returned to the owner. (This provision became meaningless when slavery was outlawed by Amendment 13 to the Constitution in 1865.)
- New states can only be added to the union if the U.S. Congress plus the legislatures of all the states agree.
- The U.S. Congress has authority over all territory which belongs to the United States. This means territory which is not a state.
- The U.S. government guarantees that all states will always have representative governments. State governments will only have the powers their people give them.
- The U.S. government promises to protect the states from invasion by any foreign country.
- If a state asks for help, the U.S. government will protect the people of any state from violence within that state.

Article 5

Article 5 tells how the Constitution can be changed. Changes in the Constitution are called **amendments**.

There are two ways an amendment to the Constitution may be **proposed** (suggested). They are:

- 2/3 of the members of both houses of the U.S. Congress may agree to propose an amendment.
- The legislatures of 2/3 of the states may call for a Constitutional Convention to propose an amendment.

After an amendment has been proposed, it must be ratified (approved). There are two ways an amendment to the U.S. Constitution may be ratified. They are:

- The legislatures of 3/4 of the states must approve the amendment.

65

- The states may call state constitutional conventions; 3/4 of these conventions must approve the amendment.

Congress decides which of the two ways will be used to approve any particular amendment which has been proposed.

Article 5 also says that no amendment to the Constitution shall ever change each state's right to have the same number of Senators as every other state. This means that even though there may be more large states than small states, the large states cannot get together and take away the power of the small states.

Article 6

Article 6 lists some general items. These are:

- Any debt which the U.S. had under the Articles of Confederation would be honored under the new Constitution.
- The U.S. Constitution is the highest law of the whole country. If a state law disagrees with the U.S. Constitution, the state law must be changed.
- All officials of local, state, and federal governments must promise to support the U.S. Constitution.
- No person shall ever be required to support any religion in order to hold office in any local or state government or in the U.S. government.

Article 7

Article 7 tells how the U.S. Constitution was to be **ratified** (approved). Nine of the original 13 states had to ratify the new Constitution before it went into effect.

Ratifying the Constitution

The U.S. Constitution was finished in September, 1787. By June, 1788, nine states had ratified it.

The tiny state of Rhode Island was the last to ratify the U.S. Constitution. The people of Rhode Island were not sure they wanted to be a part of the federal government. They were afraid that the larger states would not treat the smaller states fairly.

The people of the United States have followed the Constitution. Today, the small state of Rhode Island has the same rights as the large states do.

Think About It

1. The Preamble to the Constitution lists the reasons why the Constitution was written. Give three of these reasons.
2. What is Article 1 about?
3. What subject is covered in Article 2?
4. What is the subject of Article 3?
5. Give two ways in which Article 4 of the U.S Constitution protects the people of the states.
6. What is the subject of Article 5?
7. What guarantee does Article 5 give to protect the small states?
8. What does Article 6 say must happen if a state law disagrees with the U.S. Constitution?
9. When was the U.S. Constitution finished?
10. Why was Rhode Island afraid to ratify the U.S. Constitution?

CHAPTER 14

The Bill of Rights

When the U.S. Constitution was first written, some states worried that it did not say anything about the rights of free people. It told how the government would be organized, but it had no Bill of Rights. All of the state constitutions had a Bill of Rights.

The writers of the Constitution agreed to add a Bill of Rights to the U.S. Constitution.

> The first 10 amendments to the U.S. Constitution are called the **Bill of Rights.**

These amendments guarantee the basic rights of free people to United States citizens.

Amendment 1

Amendment 1 guarantees five basic rights of free people:

- Freedom of religion,
- Freedom of speech,
- Freedom of the press,
- Freedom to get together in groups,
- Freedom to petition the government.

Freedom of Religion

The Constitution says that the government may not get involved in any religion. Church and state must be entirely separate.

This means that the government may not support any religion with money or any other kind of aid. Such support would show favoritism and violate the separation of church and state.

Religion is an entirely private matter. You are free to have whatever religion you want—or to have no religion if you prefer.

No one can stop you from going to the church or synagogue of your choice or praying in the way you prefer.

No one can force you to follow any religious practices. No one can make you go to any church or synagogue or pray in any particular way. Also, you cannot force anyone to follow your religious practices.

Freedom of Speech and Press

You may say whatever you want as long as it doesn't hurt someone else or endanger the nation's safety.

You may also print your ideas in books and newspapers as long as you don't hurt other people or endanger the nation's safety. You may even publicly say that you disagree with the government or any government official.

Freedom to Assemble

You may get together with other people in groups. You may even have demonstrations to protest what the government does if the demonstrations are peaceful.

Freedom to Petition the Government

You may send letters to government officials to protest things which the government is doing.

You cannot be punished for disagreeing with the government or complaining to the government.

Amendment 2

Amendment 2 guarantees the right to keep weapons. It was enacted to assure the states that the federal government would not take away the state militias (National Guard). The Supreme Court has recognized the right of governments to put some limitations and restrictions on weapons for the public safety.

Amendment 3

Amendment 3 says you do not have to keep soldiers in your home in peacetime. This was important to the people in 1789 because Britain had made the colonists keep British soldiers in their homes during the French and Indian War.

The Bill of Rights guarantees that even in wartime, a special law must be passed before you would have to keep soldiers in your home.

Amendment 4

Amendment 4 keeps you free from unreasonable searches and seizures. Before the police can search you or your property, they must have

- enough information to believe that they will probably find what they are looking for, and
- a search warrant from a judge. The warrant must say exactly what place or what person the police may search.

Amendment 5

Amendment 5 protects you if you are accused of a crime.

Not everyone who is accused of a crime is guilty. If you are guilty, the law must prove your guilt fairly. If you are not guilty, the law must protect you from being punished for what you did not do.

Amendment 5 guarantees due process of law to people accused of a crime.

These are the rights which Amendment 5 gives you:

- If you are accused of a crime, a group of citizens called a **grand jury** must hear the evidence against you. The grand jury must decide if there is enough evidence to have a trial. If there is not enough evidence, the charges will be dropped.
- You may not be tried more than one time for the same thing.
- You do not have to give evidence against yourself to the police or in a trial.
- Your trial must be fair, and you must have an unbiased judge. **This is called due process of law.**

Amendment 5 also says that you must be paid a fair price if the government needs to take some of your property for public use.

Amendment 6

Amendment 6 is about **criminal law.**

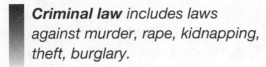
Criminal law includes laws against murder, rape, kidnapping, theft, burglary.

Amendment 6 protects your rights to defend yourself if you are on trial.

Amendment 6 guarantees a **fair trial** for people accused of crimes.

These are the rights which **Amendment 6** gives you:

- If you are accused of a crime, you may have a jury trial or you may be tried by a judge without a jury. The decision is yours.
- Your trial must take place as soon as possible after you are arrested.
- Your trial cannot be in secret. The trial must be open to the public.
- Your trial must take place in the same area where the crime was done. But it is your right to have the trial moved to another place if you think you won't get a fair trial in the place where the crime was done.
- The people on your jury must not have made up their minds about your case before the trial. This is called an **impartial** jury or an **unbiased** jury.
- You must be told plainly what you are accused of.
- You must be told who is accusing you.
- You may hear what the witnesses against you say, and you may ask these witnesses questions.
- You may have witnesses come and tell your side of the case. In fact, you have the right to force these witnesses to come to the trial even if they would rather not.
- You may have a lawyer to help you in your trial even if you do not have the money to pay a lawyer.

Amendment 7

Amendment 7 is about **civil law** trials.

Civil law deals with disputes between people about their legal rights and duties.

If you make a contract to work for someone and that person doesn't pay you, you can bring a civil case against that person. Civil law does not deal with actions which are crimes.

Amendment 7 says that if the problem in a civil case amounts to more than $20, the people involved may have a jury trial if they wish.

Amendment 8

Amendment 8 says that all bails, fines, and punishments must be fair. Punishments may not be cruel.

Amendment 9

Amendment 9 says that the rights listed in the Bill of Rights are not the only rights you have. If the Bill of Rights forgot to mention some right which free people should have, this right will not be denied to you just because it is not listed in the Bill of Rights.

Amendment 10

Amendment 10 says that the states will keep all the powers which are not given to the U.S. government and not denied to the states by the U.S. Constitution.

The **Bill of Rights** was written in 1789. Two years later, in 1791 it became part of the U.S. Constitution. All the rights listed in the Bill of Rights are guaranteed to all the people in the United States, no matter which state they live in.

Think About It

1. Why was a Bill of Rights added to the U.S. Constitution?
2. Name three basic rights of free people which are guaranteed in the First Amendment to the U.S. Constitution.
3. What do Amendments 2 and 3 guarantee?
4. How does Amendment 4 protect citizens?
5. How does Amendment 5 protect people who are accused of a crime?
6. What does **due process of law** mean?
7. Name five protections which Amendment 6 gives to people who are on trial for a crime?
8. What rights does Amendment 7 give to citizens?
9. What guarantees does Amendment 8 give to citizens?
10. What do Amendments 9 and 10 say?

CHAPTER 15

Changing Constitutions

Times change. People's needs change. Sometimes some of the laws need to change. Sometimes the way a government works needs to change, even if the government is basically a good one.

- **Some constitutions are short and to the point.** They give a general plan for government. They don't give a lot of details. These constitutions are **flexible** and don't become out-of-date quickly.
- **Other constitutions are long and detailed.** They give a lot of specific laws and try to cover every little thing. When times change, these constitutions aren't **flexible.**

State Constitutions

Most of the constitutions of the 50 states are long and have a lot of detail. They try to cover every little thing instead of just giving a general plan for government.

These constitutions are not **flexible.** They cannot keep up with changing times or with people's changing needs.

Most state constitutions have to be changed often.

- Some states change their constitutions by **writing a new constitution**. One state (Louisiana) has replaced its constitution 11 times.
- Other states change their constitutions by **amendments**. One state (Texas) has a constitution with over 300 amendments.

An **amendment** is an official change made by passing a new article.

Most state constitutions are very long. Half of the state constitutions have 20,000 words or more. One state's constitution (Georgia's) has 500,000 words.

When a constitution is this long, it is **inflexible**. It is also confusing and hard for people to understand it all. It is even hard for people to read it all!

The U.S. Constitution

The U.S. Constitution is more than 200 years old. It has only 7,000 words. The U.S. Constitution has been changed only 16 times since the Bill of Rights was added to it in 1791.

The U.S. Constitution has lasted a long time with very few amendments because it gives a general plan of government.

The U.S. Constitution is short and to the point. It doesn't go into a lot of detail. Therefore, it doesn't become out-of-date quickly.

A constitution which is very long or which has many amendments becomes very confusing to read and understand. A brief constitution which gets to the point and gives a general plan for government is flexible and much more useful to the people.

Amendments

Sometimes even a good constitution needs to be changed. Sixteen times since the original U.S. Constitution and Bill of Rights took effect, the people of the United States have changed the U.S. Constittion.

These 16 amendments can be put into three groups.

- *Group 1.* An amendment which took rights away from the people
- *Group 2.* Amendments which gave rights to more people
- *Group 3.* Amendments which changed how the government works

These amendments are listed for you. The date in parentheses after each amendment tells you when that amendment became part of the U.S. Constitution.

Group 1. An Amendment Which Took Rights Away from the People

In 1919, **Amendment 18** to the U.S. Constitution outlawed all alcoholic beverages. This amendment made it illegal to manufacture, sell, or transport any alcoholic beverages anywhere in the United States. This was called **Prohibition.**

The people who supported Prohibition were very concerned about the problems caused by alcohol. They believed that the way to solve these problems was to prohibit (outlaw) all alcohol from being made, sold, or transported in the United States. These people believed the whole country would be better off if there were no alcohol at all.

But Prohibition didn't stop people from drinking. It didn't even stop people from making and transporting alcohol. In fact, some people, called bootleggers, got rich by making and selling alcohol illegally.

Many people in the United States believed it was everyone's right to decide for himself or herself whether or not to drink. They believed that the government had no right to make this decision for the people. They believed that the people's right of **self-determination**—the right of the people to decide things for themselves—had been taken away.

In 1933, Amendment 21 repealed Prohibition. The right to decide for themselves was given back to the people.

Since then, no other amendment has ever been added to the U.S. Constitution which tried to take away the people's right to decide for themselves.

Group 2. Amendments Which Gave Rights to More People

Eight of the 16 amendments to the U.S. Constitution gave some rights to some group of people—rights which the original U.S. Constitution did not guarantee to them.

Amendment 13 (1865) gave freedom to slaves.

Amendment 14 (1868) gave citizenship to freed slaves. It also guaranteed due process of law and equal protection of the laws to every citizen, including former slaves.

Amendment 15 (1870) gave the right to vote to male freed slaves.

Amendment 19 (1920) gave the right to vote to women.

Amendment 21 (1933) gave each state the right to decide if alcoholic beverages would be legal in that state.

Amendment 23 (1961) gave people in Washington, D. C. the right to vote for President and Vice President.

Amendment 24 (1964) gave the right to vote to people who were too poor to pay a poll tax (voting tax). Some states had used this tax to keep poor ex-slaves from voting. This amendment outlawed a poll tax.

Amendment 26 (1971) gave the right to vote to people 18-20 years old.

The Right to Vote

The original U.S. Constitution did not say who could vote or who could not vote. It left this up to each state.

At first, only free, white, adult males who owned property could vote. In some places, men who didn't believe in God could not vote.

Today this has changed. In all states, every citizen over the age of 18 can vote. Constitutional amendments make sure that no one can be denied the right to vote because of his or her race or sex, no matter what state he or she lives in.

• Property and religious requirements for voting were removed by the states.

• **Black people, women, and young people above the age of 18** are guaranteed the right to vote by amendments to the U.S. Constitution.

When a right is guaranteed in the U.S. Constitution, the people in all the states must be treated the same.

Group 3. Amendments Which Changed How Government Works

Seven of the 16 amendments to the U.S. Constitution changed some part of how government works.

Amendment 11 (1798) says that a person in State A who wants to sue State B must take the case to State B's courts. Federal courts cannot handle this kind of case.

Amendment 12 (1804) changed the way Presidential Electors vote for President and Vice President.

Unit E covers the electoral process.

Amendment 16 (1913) created the Income Tax.

Amendment 17 (1913) lets the people elect U.S. Senators directly.

Before this amendment, U.S. Senators were elected by state legislatures.

Amendment 20 (1933) says that the new President and Vice President of the United States will take office on January 20 and that Congress shall meet at least once a year.

Amendment 22 (1955) says that no person may be President for more than 10 years.

Amendment 25 (1967) tells how to replace a President or Vice President who dies, resigns, or gets too sick to keep his or her job.

Think About It

1. Name three groups of people who have been guaranteed the right to vote by an amendment to the U.S. Constitution.
2. Name four amendments which gave some rights to some group of people. Tell what right was given to what group by each amendment.
3. Tell why Amendment 21, the amendment which repealed Prohibition, was passed.

UNIT C SUMMARY

The U.S. Constitution is made up of a Preamble (introduction), seven Articles, and 26 amendments.

The Preamble tells why the Constitution was written.

The seven Articles set up the three branches of government, tell how the states will relate to each other, how the Constitution may be changed, and how the Constitution was to be ratified (approved).

The first 10 Amendments to the Constitution are called the Bill of Rights. These amendments (changes) were added to the Constitution soon after it was written.

These amendments guarantee the rights of free people to all citizens of the United States.

Sixteen more amendments have been added to the Constitution in addition to the Bill of Rights. One amendment took the right to drink alcoholic beverages away from people. Eight amendments gave rights to more people. Seven amendments change some part of the way government works.

The U.S. Constitution has lasted 200 years with very few changes because it is flexible. It is short and to the point. It gives a general plan of government.

UNIT C QUIZ

*Decide whether each statement below is **true** or **false**. Write **T** or **F** on your own paper. Then write a sentence which tells **why** each false statement is false.*

___ 1. The Preamble of the U.S. Constitution tells why the Constitution was written.

___ 2. One reason why the Constitution was written was to set up a federal government which worked better than the old one did.

___ 3. One reason why the Constitution was written was to explain why the colonists wanted to break away from Britain.

___ 4. The U.S. Constitution is divided into seven parts called articles.

___ 5. Article 1 of the Constitution creates the judicial branch of government.

___ 6. Article 2 of the Constitution creates the executive branch of government.

___ 7. The Constitution provides for a legislative branch of the federal government to make laws for the United States.

___ 8. The head of the executive branch of the U.S. government is the Supreme Court.

___ 9. The judicial branch of the U.S. government settles questions about what the laws mean.

___10. The Constitution says nothing about the relation of the states to each other.

___11. The U.S. Constitution cannot be changed.

___12. The U.S. Constitution is the highest law of the whole country.

___13. The Bill of Rights was part of the original Constitution.

___14. The first 10 amendments to the Constitution are called the Preamble.

___15. Amendment 1 to the Constitution says that church and state must be entirely separate.

___16. Amendment 1 to the Constitution says that you may say whatever you please as long as you don't disagree with the government or any government official.

___17. Amendment 1 says that people in the United States are free to get together in groups.

___18. Amendment 2 gives each state the right to have a militia (National Guard).

___19. Amendment 3 says that people in the U.S. must keep soldiers in their homes even in peacetime.

___20. Amendment 4 says that the police must have a search warrant from a judge before they can search your home.

___21. Amendment 5 protects people who are accused of a crime.

___22. A grand jury must decide if there is enough evidence for an accused person to be tried.

___23. If you are arrested and you are guilty, you must tell the police what you did.

___24. If you are accused of a crime, it is your right to have a lawyer help you in your trial.

___25. Amendment 6 guarantees a fair trial for people accused of crimes.

___26. The best constitutions give a general plan of government and are flexible.

___27. Men and women were given the right to vote in the original Constitution.

___28. Male freed slaves were given the right to vote by Amendment 15.

___29. It is up to every state to decide if young people between 18 and 21 can vote.

___30. Amendment 24 says that people must pay a poll tax before they can vote.

Learning Objectives for Unit D

When you have finished this unit, you will be able to:

- Tell what group makes laws for the United States, for each state, and for local areas.

- Name some issues which city lawmakers handle.

- Tell what form of government U.S. cities have.

- Tell how state lawmakers are chosen.

- Tell how a bill becomes law in state legislatures.

- Name the houses of the U.S. Congress.

- Tell how a person might become a member of either house of the U.S. Congress.

- Tell what jobs each house of Congress may do and what jobs the two houses share.

- Tell what things the U.S. Constitution says Congress may not do.

- Tell how a bill becomes a law in the United States.

- Tell how the system of checks and balances applies to Congress.

UNIT D

THE LEGISLATIVE BRANCH OF GOVERNMENT

Most governments in the United States divide their powers among three branches—legislative, executive, and judicial.

This is called the **separation of powers**.

The lawmaking power is given to the branch called **the legislative branch.**

So far you have learned that
- people need laws;
- laws should be written down;
- the people should have some say about what the laws are.

Now you are going to learn how laws are made.

Levels of Government

The U.S. Constitution is the highest law in the United States. The U.S. Constitution

- gives a general plan of government,
- guarantees the rights of free people.

Everyone in the United States must obey what the U.S. Constitution says. But all the laws which people need are not written into the U.S. Constitution.

Laws for local areas are made by **city councils or county commissioners**.

Laws for each state are made by the **state legislatures.**

Laws for the whole country are made by the **U.S. Congress.**

CHAPTER 16

Lawmaking in Local Governments

Local governments take care of the everyday services which people need.

Counties

Almost all of the 50 states are divided into counties. The people in each county elect representatives to be members of their county board. These representatives are usually called **commissioners** or **supervisors.**

County commissioners have very few legislative duties. Their main job is to administer (carry out) state laws. Some of the legislative jobs of county commissioners are to

- decide on county tax rates;
- decide how much tax money to spend on each of the county's needs;
- make rules to protect public health.

Cities

Most local laws are made by city governments. Cities get their power to exist from their state legislatures. The state legislature must issue the city a **charter.** The charter is the city's constitution.

The city's charter tells what form of government the city will have. Not all city governments are exactly the same. But all cities have representative governments. All cities elect officials to make their laws

and run the day-to-day business of government.

The lawmakers for most cities are called **city council** members.

■ *City laws are called **ordinances.***

Yourtown, U.S.A.

The year is 19??. The place is Yourtown. You are 25 years old, and you have just been elected to Yourtown's City Council.

The election was held last week. You were really glad to get it over with. After all, you'd been campaigning for almost three months.

Campaigning—long hours of meeting people, talking with people, speaking to clubs and civic groups, organizing rallies, handing out leaflets telling about yourself and your views.

But all that work paid off. The people of Yourtown understood your sincerity. They believed in your ability to do a good job. More people voted for you than for your opponent. You got over 16,000 votes. Your opponent got only about 11,000 votes.

16,000 votes. In a town as large as Yourtown, that doesn't seem like very many. In fact, all the votes cast for you and your opponent put together were only 27,000. That's only about a quarter of all the voters in Yourtown. Is it true that only one quarter of the people of Yourtown care who makes their laws and other political decisions?

In your crowded office today, it seems that everyone in Yourtown cares. You have had phone calls all morning, and your office is full of people who want to tell you their opinions.

Tomorrow the five City Council members from Yourtown will meet and vote on a very important matter. Many people in the town will be affected by the decision of the City Council. Now, even people who didn't vote want to tell the Council members their opinion.

The Issue

Yourtown has been growing. New people and new businesses have moved to town. Yourtown has more cars now than ever before. In fact, Yourtown has so many cars that traffic is a mess. When people want to go downtown, they can't find any place to park.

The City Council has suggested this solution:

The city should build two large parking buildings near the downtown area. One would be on the east side of downtown; the other would be on the west side. The city would have a shuttle bus to take people from the parking buildings to the stores and businesses downtown.

The downtown streets should be closed to cars. Only pedestrians and bicycles and the city's shuttle busses would be allowed downtown.

As the hours go by, you listen to many people's views. You hear what the business people think. You hear what the people who work in downtown stores and offices think. You hear what shoppers think. You hear what taxpayers think. You even hear from a company which wants to sell the city some shuttle buses.

Soon you must make a decision. You must cast your vote with the other City Council members. Your vote will help decide what the city will do about its traffic problem. Your decision will affect many people in Yourtown.

Other Issues

Traffic is just one of many issues which City Councils deal with. Here are a few more:

Water. Is there enough water for everyone? Is the water safe to drink?

Police. Are there enough police officers to protect the people?

Fire protection. Are there enough fire fighters? Is their equipment up-to-date?

Garbage. Does the city have a good system for keeping things clean?

Public buildings. Does the city need a new school? a new hospital? a new jail?

Taxes. How will the city pay for all its needs? Are new taxes needed?

Transportation. Does the city need a public bus or subway system?

Parks. The City Council runs the city parks and the city's recreation programs.

Permits. A citizens' group wants to hold a rally and demonstration in the city park. The City Council must give them a permit.

Zoning. In some cities, the City Council decides which part of the city will be used for different purposes. This is called zoning. Different parts of the city are zoned for industry, stores, houses, or hospitals, for example.

Think About It

1. What is the main job of county commissioners?
2. What are some of the legislative jobs county commissioners do?
3. What forms of government do U.S. cities have?
4. From whom do cities get their power to exist?
5. What are city laws called?
6. Name eight issues which city lawmakers deal with.

CHAPTER 17 Lawmaking in State Governments

Each state has a constitution which divides the powers of state government into three branches.

> The **legislative branch** of each state's government makes laws for that state.

Everyone in a particular state must obey the laws of that state. The laws of one state may be different from the laws of another state, but no state's laws may go against the U.S. Constitution.

State Legislatures

> The legislative branch of each state is called its **legislature.**

The legislatures of all the states are not exactly the same. But all have members who are elected by the voters of that state. These lawmakers are called **state legislators.**

All the states except one have two houses in their legislature. One house is called the state senate. Its members are called state senators.

The other house is called either the house of representatives, the assembly, the general assembly, or the house of delegates.

Members of this house are called state representatives or members of the assembly.

One state, Nebraska, has only one house in its state legislature.

Who May Be a State Legislator?

Each state sets its own requirements for its legislators. In some states anyone over the age of 18 may be a representative. In other states the minimum age is 21.

State senators usually must be at least 25 years old. In some states, state senators must bc 30 years old.

All state legislators must be U.S. citizens and must live in the area where they are elected.

How Long Do State Legislators Serve?

The term for state legislators is set by each state's constitution. In most states, state senators serve for four years. In some states, state senators serve only two years.

In most states, state representatives serve two years. In a few states, state representatives serve four years.

Who Is the Presiding Officer in State Legislatures?

The members of each state's house of representatives elect one of their own members to be the presiding officer. This person is called the **speaker of the house.**

In most states, the presiding officer of the state senate is the **lieutenant governor**. The lieutenant governor is elected by the voters of the state and is a member of the executive branch of state government. In a few states, the state senators elect their presiding officer from among their own members.

How Often Do State Legislatures Meet?

Some state legislatures meet every year; others meet every two years. Sessions usually last two to three months.

Powers of State Legislatures

The U.S. (federal) government shares many powers with state governments. In Unit 3 you learned that Amendment 10 of the U.S. Constitution gives states any powers **except**

- those which belong to the federal government and
- those which the U.S. Constitution specifically denies to the states.

Things State Lawmakers May Do
- Make laws for their state.
- Set up local governments.
- Set up state and local courts.
- Collect taxes.
- Vote on the state's budget.

Things States May Not Do
The U.S. Constitution says that states **may not do** certain things which no democratic government should do.

State legislatures may never
- make an act a crime **after** the act is done;

- make a law to punish a person without giving the person a trial;
- pass a law saying that a contract will not be honored. States must honor contracts.
- give anyone a title of nobility;
- coin money.

Unless Congress approves, states may not:
- tax imports (goods coming from another country) or exports (goods being sent to another country);
- keep troops or warships in peace time;
- make an agreement with another state or with a foreign country;
- go to war unless invaded.

Amendments to the U.S. Constitution say states may not:
- permit slavery (Amendment 13);
- deny equal privileges to any citizen (Amendment 14);
- deny equal protection of the law to any citizen (Amendment 14);
- deny due process of law to any citizen (Amendment 14);
- deny any citizen the right to vote because of
  - race (Amendment 15),
  - sex (Amendment 19), or
  - age, if 18 or over (Amendment 26).

You may read about the legislative branch of government in the states in **Article 1, Section 10**, of the U.S. Constitution.

Think About It

1. Name the branch of state government which makes laws for the state.
2. What is your state's legislature called? How many members does it have? How often does it meet?
3. How many houses do most state legislatures have?
4. How long is the term for state representatives in your state?
5. How long is the term for state senators in your state?
6. What is the title of the presiding officer in a state's house of representatives?
7. What is the title of the presiding officer in a state's senate?
8. Name four things which state lawmakers do.
9. Name eight things which state legislatures may never do.

CHAPTER 18

How Laws Are Made In State Legislatures

1. A **bill** (proposed law) is introduced in one house of the state legislature.

2. A **committee** (small group of legislators) studies the bill.

3. The committee votes on the bill. If the committee approves the bill (majority vote), the bill goes to the entire house.

4. The entire house debates the bill.

5. The entire house votes on the bill. If the house approves the bill by a simple majority vote (over 1/2), the bill goes to the other house.

6. Steps 1-4, above, are followed in the second house of the state legislature.

7. The second house votes on the bill. If the bill is approved by the second house **in the same form as the first house approved it,** the bill is sent to the governor to be signed.

8. If the two houses approve different versions of the bill, a **Conference Committee** must work out a compromise. Then both houses must vote again to approve one single version of the bill. A simple majority vote is needed.

9. The bill then goes to the governor to be signed.

10. The governor in every state except North Carolina has the power to veto a bill. **Veto** means to say **no**—to turn a bill down.

11. If a bill is vetoed, the legislature may **override** the veto by voting on the bill again. In most states, a 2/3 vote of both houses is needed to override a governor's veto. Some states require only a simple majority vote in both houses.

12. Once a bill has been approved by the governor, or passed by the legislature over the governor's veto, it becomes a **law.**

Bills in Committee

Every bill introduced in a state's legislature must first go to a committee. Committees are made up of members of the legislative house. Committee members are chosen in different ways in different states.

A committee is a very dangerous place for a bill. Most bills **die in committee.**

> To **die in committee** means that the bill never gets out of the committee.

Here is how the committee process works.

When a committee gets a bill, the committee members have a choice. They may

- ignore the bill and let it die;
- talk about the bill and send it back to their house in the same form that it came to them;
- make changes in the bill and then send it back to their house.

Most bills never get out of committee.

Very, very few bills are sent back to the house unchanged.

Most bills which come back to the house from committee have been changed from their original form.

All bills which are introduced into either house of the legislature must first go to a committee. If the committee doesn't want to send the bill back to their house, the rest of the members of that house may never even get a chance to vote on that bill.

Different states have different ways to handle this situation. Find out what the legislature in your state does when a committee tries to kill a bill which the rest of the legislators want to vote on.

The Conference Committee

Before a bill can become a law in any state, both houses of that state's legislature must pass the **same bill**. If the bill passed by the second house of the state's legislature is different in any way from the bill passed by the first house, the bill cannot be sent to the governor for signature.

When two different versions of the same bill are passed by the two houses of a state's legislature, a **Conference Committee** must meet to work out a compromise bill.

A few members of each house of the legislature get together and form the **Conference Committee**. After they have worked out a compromise bill, the new bill is sent back to both houses of the state legislature. Both houses must approve the compromise bill before it can be sent to the governor for signature.

Think About It

1. What is the difference between a bill and a law?
2. Tell how a bill becomes law in your state's legislature.
3. Tell why a committee is a dangerous place for a bill.
4. What is the purpose of a Conference Committee?

CHAPTER 19

Lawmaking in the Federal Government

The U.S. Congress

Congress is the lawmaking body of the federal government.

Congress has two houses (small h).

- The **House of Representatives** is the larger of these two houses. It is sometimes called the **House** (capital H).
- The **Senate** is the smaller of the two houses of Congress.

The job of Congress is to pass laws for the United States. When a law is first suggested, it is called a **bill**. Most bills may be started in either house of Congress, that is, in either the **House** or the **Senate**. But a bill must pass both houses to become law.

In all of Congress, there are 535 members. These members are called **Congresspersons.**

All Congresspersons are elected by the people of their state. Elections for Congresspersons are always held in November of even-numbered years. This election is called the **general election**. The term of office for Congresspersons always begins on January 3 of the next year.

> You may read about the legislative branch of government in **Article 1** of the U.S. Constitution.

The House of Representatives

Number of members—**435**
Members are called—**Representatives**
Presiding officer—**Speaker of the House**

Suppose you want to be a representative

- You must be at least 25 years old.
- You must have been a U.S. citizen for at least 7 years.
- You must live in the state where you are elected.

The 435 representatives are divided up among the 50 states according to population. Each representative represents one district within his or her state. The smallest state has one representative. The largest state has 43 representatives.

Term of Office

Representatives are elected for 2-year terms. That means every two years you must be re-elected. You may be re-elected as many times as the voters of your district want to elect you.

Presiding Officer

The presiding officer of the U.S. House of Representatives is called the **Speaker of the House**. The Speaker is elected by all the members of the House from among the members of the House. Usually the Speaker is someone who has been a representative for a long time.

Jobs Which Only the House of Representatives May Do

- Start **tax bills.**
- Bring charges of **impeachment.**
- Elect a President if the electoral college doesn't give any candidate a majority vote. (You will study the electoral college in Unit E.)

Start Tax Bills

Most bills may start in either the House or the Senate. **Tax bills may only start in the House.** This is because there are more members in the House, and these members are closer to the people.

Each representative represents fewer people than senators do. The writers of the U.S. Constitution decided that only the House could start tax bills. This gives the people more control over tax laws.

Bring Charges of Impeachment

Impeachment *means accusing a government official of some wrongdoing.*

If the members of the House believe that some government official is doing something wrong, they may vote a **bill of impeachment.**

After the House votes a bill of impeachment (that is, brings charges), the accused official must be tried by the Senate.

If the Senate finds the official guilty, the official must leave office.

Think About It

1. What is the name of the lawmaking body of the United States government?
2. Name the two houses of the U.S. Congress.
3. Which house is the larger?
4. Which house is the smaller?
5. What are the members of the House of Representatives called?
6. How long do the members of the House of Representatives serve?
7. What are the Constitutional qualifications for members in the House of Representatives?
8. Name three special powers which the Constitution gives to the House of Representatives.
9. Why does the Constitution give the House of Representatives the power to start tax bills?
10. What does impeachment mean?
11. What is the role of the House of Representatives in an impeachment?
12. What is the role of the Senate in an impeachment?

The Senate

Number of members—**100**
Members are called—**Senators**
Presiding officer—**Vice President of the United States**

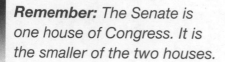

Remember: The Senate is one house of Congress. It is the smaller of the two houses.

Suppose you want to be a Senator.

- You must be at least 30 years old.
- You must have been a United States citizen for at least 9 years.
- You must live in the state where you are elected.

Term of Office

Senators are elected for 6-year terms. You may be re-elected senator as many times as the voters of your state want to re-elect you.

Senators have overlapping terms. This means that all senators are not elected at the same time. Every two years, 1/3 of the senators are elected.

The following table shows how overlapping terms work. A senator who is elected in 1990 takes office in 1991 and will serve until 1997. A senator who is elected in 1992 takes office in 1993 and will serve until 1999.

Four of the six years of this second Senator's term will overlap the term of the first Senator.

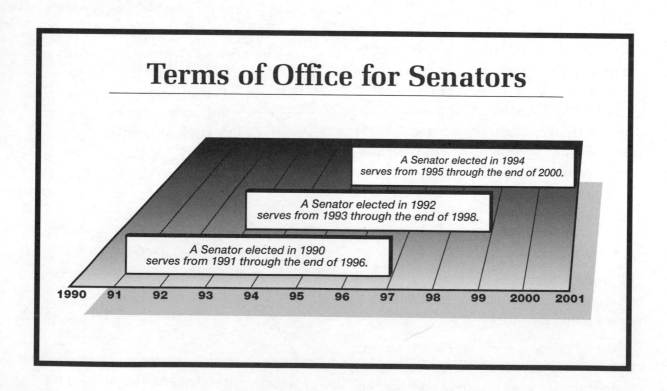

Terms of Office for Senators

A Senator elected in 1994 serves from 1995 through the end of 2000.

A Senator elected in 1992 serves from 1993 through the end of 1998.

A Senator elected in 1990 serves from 1991 through the end of 1996.

1990 91 92 93 94 95 96 97 98 99 2000 2001

The 100 senators are divided equally among the states. Each state has two senators, no matter how many people live in that state.

In the House of Representatives, all the people of the United States have equal representation. In the Senate, all the states have equal representation.

**Jobs Which Only
the U.S. Senate May Do**

- Say yes or no to the appointments which the President makes. This includes the President's appointment of Justices of the Supreme Court. This is called **approving** appointments.

- Say yes or no to the treaties which the President makes with other governments. This is called **ratifying** treaties.

- Hold a **trial** for government officials who are **impeached** (accused of wrongdoing) by the House of Representatives.

- Elect a Vice President for the United States if the electoral college doesn't give any candidate a majority vote. (You will learn about the electoral college in Unit E.)

Think About It

1. How many members are there in the U.S. Senate?
2. What are members of the Senate called?
3. Who is the presiding officer of the U.S. Senate?
4. How long is the term of a U.S. Senator?
5. Are all members of the U.S. Senate elected at the same time?
6. What is meant by overlapping terms?
7. Each state has how many senators?
8. Name four jobs which only the U.S. Senate may do.

Powers Shared by Both Houses of Congress

Jobs Which Congress May Do

Remember: **Congress** means both the House of Representatives and the Senate.

Most of Congress' powers are **shared by both houses**. One house cannot do something without the approval of the other house.

Sharing power between the two houses is part of the **system of checks and balances**. It keeps power balanced between the two houses. Neither house can have too much power.

91

The **legislative branch** of the federal government has more different powers than any of the other branches. This is because all the members of this branch are elected by the people. The people have more direct control over Congresspersons than they do over members of the other branches of government.

Here are some of the powers which the U.S. Constitution gives to Congress.

- Collect taxes to pay the costs of running the federal government.
- Coin money for the United States.
- Make rules for trade between the states and for trade with other countries.
- Provide for the defense of the United States.
- Raise and support armies and a navy.
- Declare war.
- Set up a Post Office system.
- Set standards for weights and measures in the United States.
- Set up federal courts which have less power than the Supreme Court.

- Provide for the general welfare of the United States.
- Make all laws which are necessary and proper for carrying out Congress' constitutional powers.

You may read about the powers of Congress in the U.S. Constitution, **Article 1, Section 8.**

The "Elastic Clause"

The writers of the Constitution knew that as the years went by, the needs of the country would change. They didn't try to cover every single thing in the Constitution. Instead, they gave Congress the power to **"make all laws which are necessary and proper"** for carrying out Congress' constitutional powers.

*This clause is called the **elastic clause** or Congress' **implied powers.***

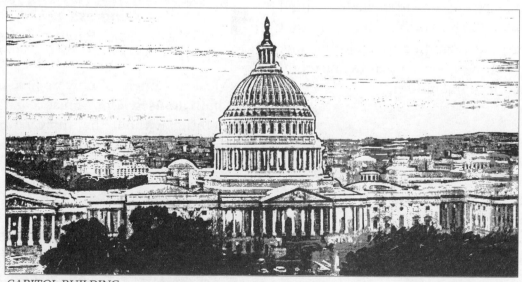

CAPITOL BUILDING
Both Houses of the Congress meet in this building. Can you name them? Can you list some of the powers which the Houses share?

The elastic clause makes our U.S. Constitution flexible. It has allowed the U.S. Constitution to stretch to keep up with the changing needs of our growing population and our new technology.

The elastic clause allowed Congress to create an air force, even though the Constitution didn't mention an air force. In fact, when the Constitution was written, no one even dreamed that there would ever be airplanes!

Since the Constitution gave Congress the power to provide for the defense of the United States and set up armies, this power was stretched to include an air force when planes were invented.

A Strong Central Government

The writers of the U. S. Constitution knew that the United States needed a strong central government to help the states work together and to prevent confusion.

That is why they gave Congress the power to do a variety of things for the whole country.

Congress can
- coin money for the whole country,
- set up a Post Office for the whole country, and
- provide for the defense of the whole country.

Things Which Congress May Not Do

The U.S. Constitution put some limits on the kinds of laws which Congress may pass. The writers of the Constitution wanted to be sure that the rights of the people were protected. They also wanted to be sure that the rights of the states were protected.

The U.S. Constitution says that Congress **may not** pass laws which would

- deny a prisoner the right to be brought before a judge so that the judge can decide if the prisoner is being held lawfully;
- punish a person without having a trial;
- make some action a crime **after** the action was done;
- tax goods which are exported from one state to another;
- favor one state over another state;
- give a person a title of nobility.

You may read about these rules in **Article 1, Section 9** of the U.S. Constitution.

Think About It

1. Name eight powers which the Constitution gives to Congress.
2. What is the elastic clause?
3. Why is the elastic clause important to our government?
4. Why did the writers of the Constitution provide for a strong central government?
5. Name five things which the Constitution says that Congress may not do.

CHAPTER 20

How a Bill Becomes Law in the United States

1. A bill is introduced in either house of Congress. (Except, tax bills must start in the House of Representatives.)

2. The bill goes to a small group of lawmakers in that house to be studied. The group is called a committee. There are many committees in each house. Each committee deals with laws on a particular subject.

3. A majority of the committee members must agree to the bill and vote to send it back to their house of Congress.

4. The entire house debates the bill.

5. The entire house votes on the bill. If a majority of the members of this house approve the bill, it goes to the other house of Congress.

6. The first four steps above are followed in the second house of Congress.

7. The second house votes on the bill.
   a. If the same version of the bill is passed by a majority of the second house, the bill goes to the President to be signed.
   b. If the two houses approve different versions of the bill, it goes to a **Conference Committee** made up of members of both houses. The Conference Committee must work out a compromise. Then both houses must vote again to approve one single version of the bill.

8. A bill which has been passed by both houses of Congress then goes to the President to be signed. The President has three choices of what to do with the bill:
   a. Sign the bill. It then becomes a **law.**
   b. **Pocket veto** (hold) the bill. If Congress is in session at the end of 10 days, the bill becomes a **law**. If Congress is not in session at the end of 10 days, the bill dies.
   c. **Veto** (turn down) the bill.

9. If the President vetoes a bill, it still may have a chance to become a law.
   a. The members of both houses of Congress may vote to override the veto (pass a bill over the President's veto). To override a veto, 2/3 of the members of both houses must vote for the bill. Originally, only a majority of the members of both houses had to vote for the bill. Getting a 2/3 vote for a bill is much harder than getting a simple majority (1/2) vote.

You may read about how a bill becomes law in the United States in the U.S. Constitution, **Article 1, Section 7.**

Bills in Committees in the U.S. Congress

A committee of Congress is just as dangerous for a bill as a committee in a state legislature. Most bills die in committee.

Just as in state legislatures, committees in Congress have a choice about how to deal with bills.

The committee may

- ignore the bill and let it die;
- talk about the bill and send it back to their house in the same form as they got it;
- make changes in the bill and then send it back to their house.

All bills introduced into either house of Congress must first go to a committee. If the committee doesn't want to send the bill back to their house, the rest of the members of that house usually never even get a chance to vote on the bill. The committee has a lot of power.

- Very, very few bills are sent back to the house unchanged.
- Most bills which come back to the house from committee have been changed from their original form.
- **Most bills** never get out of committee.

Suppose the members of a committee decide to ignore a bill and let it die. *Is there anything the other members of their house can do about this?*

The answer is yes, but it is not easy.

If half the members of the entire house are interested in a bill which a committee is keeping, these members may vote to take the bill out of the committee. This doesn't happen very often because it is difficult to get half of the members of the house to agree to this action.

The Conference Committee

Before a bill can become law in the United States, a majority of both houses of Congress must pass the **same** bill. The bill passed by the House and the Senate must be the same **in every way**. If the committee in the House makes one change in the original bill, the committee in the Senate must accept the bill with this same change. Otherwise, the bill cannot be sent to the President to be signed.

If the House of Representatives passes one form of a bill and the Senate passes a different form of that bill, what can be done? Does the bill just die right there? Not necessarily.

If the two houses of Congress pass different forms of a bill, a **Conference Committee** is chosen. Half of the members of a Conference Committee are from the Senate. Half the members are from the House. Together these senators and representatives work out a compromise bill which both houses can accept.

After a compromise is reached by the Conference Committee, the new form of the bill is voted on by both houses of Congress. If both houses vote for the new bill, it is then sent to the President to be signed.

A Special Power of the Senate

When a bill is being debated in the Senate, members of the Senate have a special power—which members of the House do *not* have—called **filibuster.**

> To **filibuster** is to try to kill a bill by talking it to death.

After a bill comes back from its committee, the members of the entire house of Congress debate the bill. Members who support the bill tell why they think everyone should vote for the bill. Members who do not like the bill tell why they think it is a bad bill.

In the House of Representatives each member has a chance to talk about the bill. But the Rules Committee of the House may put a limit on how long each representative may talk about a bill. This keeps things moving in the House so that the members can get more work done.

No one in the Senate can tell a senator how long he or she may talk about a bill. While a senator is talking about a bill, the members of the Senate cannot vote on that bill or get any other work done. If some senator doesn't like a bill and is afraid that the bill may get a majority vote in the Senate, that senator has a right to keep talking as long as he or she wants to. The senator may talk about the bill or about anything that comes to his or her mind.

In the 1950s, Congress tried to pass laws guaranteeing civil rights to black people in the United States. These civil rights included the right to

- go to school with everyone else;
- eat in any restaurant;
- go to public parks and ride on public buses; and

- have a fair chance to get a good job no matter what the color of their skin was.

Some senators didn't want these civil rights laws to be passed. But they knew that more than half of the senators would vote for these bills. So a few senators decided to filibuster. They talked about the bills. They talked about the weather. They even read recipes for chicken soup to the members of the Senate. These few senators kept civil rights laws from being passed in the United States until 1957.

Stopping a Filibuster

Stopping a filibuster is very difficult. A Senate rule says that three-fifths of the senators present must vote to limit debate on a particular bill before a filibuster can be stopped. When 3/5 of the senators vote this way, it is called **closure.**

After a vote for closure, no senator may talk for more than an hour on the bill. But it is very difficult to get 3/5 of the senators to agree on one particular bill. When a bill is filibustered, it usually dies.

Checks and Balances

The writers of the U.S. Constitution divided the government into **three branches** to keep any one part of government from getting too much power.

They also created a **system of checks and balances** as another way to keep any one branch from getting too much power.

The **system of checks and balances** means that each branch can stop (check) or change actions of the other branches.

If an action of one branch threatens our system of government, the other two branches have the power to stop or change the bad action of the one branch.

**To keep either house
from having too much power:**

- Both houses of Congress must pass the **same version** of a bill. If different forms of a bill are passed in each house, a **Conference Committee** meets to work out a compromise.
- The House may **impeach** (accuse) a government official, but the Senate must find the official guilty before the official can be removed from office.

**To keep Congress from having
more power than the other
two branches of government:**

- The President must sign a bill before it can become law. If the President doesn't want to sign a bill, he or she may **veto** it.
- The Supreme Court may declare a law passed by Congress to be **unconstitutional**. This means that the law cannot continue to be a law.

**To let Congress check the other
two branches of government:**

- Congress may **amend** the Constitution.
- Congress may **override** the President's veto.
- The Senate must **approve** the officials appointed by the President. This includes Justices of the Supreme Court who are appointed by the President.
- The Senate must **ratify** (approve) treaties which the President makes with other governments.

President John F. Kennedy is shown signing a bill in 1962 before members of his cabinet and leaders of the Senate and House of Representatives. How is this an example of Checks and Balances?

Checks and Balances—Some Examples

Example 1.

Suppose you are a representative in the House. You and some of the other representatives decide to pass a tax bill which will increase everyone's income tax.

Some of the other representatives don't like this bill, but after a lot of debate a vote is taken. Your tax bill gets just over half the votes in the House. The bill passes.

Now the bill must go to the Senate. Only the House may start a tax bill, but both houses of Congress must agree to it.

The senators do not like your bill. They believe that your bill raises taxes too much. The Senate passes a bill which raises taxes, but only by a small amount.

A tax bill has now been passed by both the House and the Senate. But the two houses have not passed the **same** tax bill. Each bill is a little different.

What happens next?

The two tax bills must now go to a **Conference Committee**. Five representatives and five senators meet and talk about the bills.

After the Conference Committee agrees on a compromise, both the House and the Senate must vote again. If the House and the Senate both accept the compromise bill with at least a simple majority vote, the bill can now go to the President for his or her signature.

The Senate has **checked** (stopped) an action of the House.

The senators believed that your tax bill which was passed by the House was not good for the country. They said, *"No, you cannot pass this bill. You must first listen to our opinions. Then we must compromise."*

This is one way in which the **system of checks and balances** works in Congress.

Example 2.

You are a member of the House of Representatives. You and the other representatives learn that the President has done something illegal.

You and the other representatives have talked with the President about his actions. He doesn't believe his actions are illegal. So you and the other representatives decide he must be **impeached.**

The members of the House vote a **bill of impeachment**. This means that the President has now **officially** been accused of doing something illegal.

Next, the members of the Senate must hold a **trial**. If the senators decide that the President is guilty of the illegal actions, then he must leave office. If he is not found guilty, the charges will be dropped and he will stay in office.

Impeachment and **trial** are another way in which the **system of checks and balances** works in the U.S. government.

Think About It

1. Tell how a bill becomes law in the United States.
2. Why is a committee a dangerous place for a bill?
3. What is a **Conference Committee**? When does a bill go to a Conference Committee?
4. What is a **veto**?
5. What does **overriding a veto** mean?
6. What is a **filibuster**? Who may filibuster?
7. How does the **system of checks and balances** apply to the legislative branch of the federal government?

UNIT D SUMMARY

Laws are rules made by governments which people must obey. The U.S. Constitution is the highest law in the United States, but it doesn't include all the laws which people need.

- Laws for local areas are made by **city councils or county commissioners.**
- Laws for each state are made by the **state legislatures.**
- Laws for the whole country are made by **Congress.**

Lawmakers at all levels of government are elected by the voters. If the voters do not like the way these lawmakers do their job, the voters may elect someone else at the next election.

Local governments take care of the day-to-day business of government. City councils pass city laws called ordinances. County commissioners or supervisors have limited law-making powers, although they make some rules about such things as tax rates and spending or public health.

State laws are made by the state legislature. Each state's constitution makes the rules for its legislature. All but one of the states have two houses in their legislature.

Each state legislature makes its own laws, but the laws of all states must agree with the U.S. Constitution. Article 1, Section 10 of the U.S. Constitution gives some specific things which state lawmakers cannot do. This is to be sure that all states respect the rights of free people.

Article 1 of the U.S. Constitution establishes Congress. Congress has two houses—the Senate and the House of Representatives. Together, these two houses make laws for the United States.

Article 1 controls what Congress does. It lists things which Congress may and may not do. Article 1 also has an elastic clause which makes the Constitution flexible. The implied powers in this elastic clause let Congress do things which are "necessary and proper" to run the country, even if these things are not specifically mentioned in the Constitution.

The way a bill becomes a law is similar in both the state legislatures and Congress. Bills are studied in committees, then discussed and voted on in both houses.

Disagreements between the two houses about a bill are settled in a Conference Committee. Finally, the bill must be signed into law by the governor (for state laws) or the President (for U.S. laws).

A system of checks and balances makes sure that neither house of Congress has too much power. The system of checks and balances also keeps each of the three branches of government from having too much power. The system of checks and balances gives each branch of government ways to stop (check) or change actions of the other branches. Checks and balances are very important in protecting our democratic government.

UNIT D QUIZ

*Decide whether each statement below is **true** or **false**. Write **T** or **F** on your own paper. Then write a sentence which tells **why** each false statement is false.*

___ 1. The U.S. Constitution is the highest law in the United States.

___ 2. All the laws for all the states are written in the U.S. Constitution.

___ 3. The U.S. Congress makes laws for the whole United States.

___ 4. Laws for each state are made by state legislators.

___ 5. The main job for county commissioners is to make laws for their county.

___ 6. All cities in the United States have representative governments.

___ 7. City laws are called ordinances.

___ 8. The rules for all state legislatures are exactly the same.

___ 9. A state legislature may pass any law it wants to.

___10. After a bill is introduced in a state legislature, the bill is studied by a committee.

___11. Both houses of a state's legislature must approve the exact same form of a bill.

___12. A bill from a state legislature must be signed by the President before it can become a law.

___13. State legislatures have the power to override a veto.

___14. Most bills introduced in state legislatures die in committee.

___15. The U.S. Senate is the larger of the two houses of Congress.

___16. Members of the U.S. Congress are called Congresspersons.

___17. The U.S. House of Representatives has 435 members.

___18. The presiding officer of the U.S. House of Representatives is the Vice President of the United States.

___19. All representatives serve 4-year terms of office.

___20. All states have the same number of representatives.

___21. Only the House of Representatives may start tax bills.

___22. Impeachment means accusing a government official of some wrong-doing.

___23. All states have two U.S. Senators.

___24. All senators must be re-elected every two years.

___25. Only the U.S. Congress may de-clare war.

___26. The Senate must approve treaties and appointments made by the President.

___27. The elastic clause makes the U.S. Constitution flexible.

___28. Congress may pass a law making an action a crime after the action has been done.

___29. A Conference Committee works out a compromise if the Senate and the House pass different forms of a bill.

___30. A filibuster is a way to kill a bill by continuing to talk so that the Senate cannot vote.

Learning Objectives for Unit E

When you have finished this unit, you will be able to:

- Name the **chief executive officer** at each level of government.
- Name some important departments which carry on the day-to-day business of most cities.
- Name some important elected officials of county government.
- Name the main function of county governments.
- Tell what a **plural executive** system is.
- Tell how the President of the United States is chosen.
- Explain the major problems of the **electoral college.**
- List the main powers and duties of the President of the United States.
- Explain how the **system of checks and balances** works in the executive branch of the federal government.
- Tell what the President's **Cabinet** is.
- Tell what the **federal bureaucracy** is.

UNIT E

THE EXECUTIVE BRANCH OF GOVERNMENT

You have learned that the lawmaking powers of government are given to the legislative branch. This is true at all levels of government—local governments, state governments, and the federal government. This arrangement is part of the separation of powers.

The same arrangement is true of another branch of government—the **executive branch.** At all levels of government in the United States, **executive** officials and **executive** departments **enforce laws** and **carry on the day-to-day business of government.**

In this unit you will learn about the **executive branch** of governments.

- You will learn who **enforces** the laws made by city councils, state legislatures, and the United States Congress.
- You will also learn who **carries out** all the day-to-day business of these governments.

CHAPTER 21

The Executive Branch of Local Governments

Cities

Cities in the United States have a variety of executive systems. In most cities, an elected **mayor** is the chief executive official. Some cities hire a **city manager** to run their city government. But whatever the chief executive official of a city is called, most of the work of running the city is done by the city's **departments**. Each department handles a different part of the city's day-to-day business.

Some of the departments which most cities have are:

Police Department
Fire Department
Garbage Collection Department
Parks and Recreation Department
Health Department

Each city department is run by a **department head** or **chief**. Heads of departments may be appointed by the mayor or by the city council.

Counties

In Unit D you learned that almost all of the 50 states are divided into **counties**. The people in each county elect representatives to be members of their **county board**. These representatives are usually called **commissioners** or **supervisors**.

This picture shows a policeman, fireman, sanitation worker, and a city tax collector—all of them city workers.

County commissioners have both **legislative** and **executive** powers. Usually, there is no real separation of powers at the county level. The county board hires and supervises heads of county departments. Each department handles a different part of the county's needs.

Some county departments which most counties have are:

Road-building Department
Fire Department
Health Department
Sheriff's Department

County commissioners are elected by the voters of their county. Most counties also elect many other county officials.

Some elected officials which most counties have are:

County Clerk. The county clerk keeps records for the county. These records include birth certificates, death certificates, marriage certificates, automobile titles, deeds to property.

County Treasurer. The county treasurer receives all county money and pays the county's bills.

County Assessor. The county assessor decides the value of all the buildings and land in the county. County taxes are based on property values.

County Tax Collector. The county tax collector collects taxes for the county.

County Attorney. The county attorney prosecutes people who are accused of crimes in the county.

Constable. The constable enforces civil laws in the county.

Sheriff. The sheriff enforces criminal laws for the county. Most counties also have a number of **deputy sheriffs** to help the sheriff.

What Laws Do County Officials Enforce?

You learned in Unit D that county commissioners have very little law-making power. Most of the laws which county officials enforce are **state laws.**

> The main job of county officials is to enforce state laws and run the government of the state.

States have counties so that government can be run at the local level. This means that the officials who run the various programs of state government are much closer to the people they serve than if all the state's programs were run from the state capital.

Think About It

1. Does your city have a mayor? a city manager?
2. How many departments are there in your city's government? Make a list of them.
3. Name five elected officials which most counties have, not including the county commissioners. Tell what major job each official does.
4. What is the main job of county government within each state?

CHAPTER 22

The Executive Branch of State Governments

Governor

The **governor** is the chief executive officer in each state. In every state, the governor is elected by the voters. In most states, the governor's term of office is four years. In a few states, the governor serves a 2-year term.

The powers of the governor are different in every state.

Some of the powers which many state governors have are:

- See that state laws are carried out.
- Appoint heads of departments, members of state boards, judges of state courts.
- Draw up the state's budget.
- Sign or veto bills passed by the state legislature.
- Recommend laws to the state legislature.
- Call special sessions of the state legislature.
- Grant pardons to people convicted of crimes in that state.
- Reduce the penalty of people convicted of crimes in that state.

Lieutenant Governor

The **lieutenant governor** is also elected by the voters of each state. The lieutenant governor replaces a governor who is away or who dies or resigns. In many states, the lieutenant governor is the presiding officer of the state senate.

Plural Executive

In many states, several executive officials are elected by the voters. The governor usually has no control over these other elected officials. This is called a **plural executive** system.

A plural executive system has both good points and bad points.

Two main **good points** are:

- Executive powers of state government are spread among several people instead of being in one person's hands.
- Voters choose more than one of the people who make decisions for the state. Voters have some control over what these officials do. Officials must listen to the voters if they want to be re-elected in the next election.

Two main **bad points** are:

- The executive branch may not have much unity.
- The people may not know who is really to blame for any one problem.

Most people think the governor is head of the state's executive branch. If something goes wrong, people blame the governor. But if a state has a plural executive, the governor is head of state government in name only and is not responsible for everything that goes on in the state. The governor has little control over what other elected executive officials do.

Other Executive Officials

Listed below are three other state executive officials. In some states these officials are appointed by the governor. In other states these officials are elected by the voters of the state.

Secretary of State
- keeps records for the state
- publishes the laws passed by the state legislature
- makes rules for state elections

Attorney General
- represents the state in court cases
- gives legal advice to state officials

State Treasurer
- collects taxes and pays the bills for the state
  (This office has different names in different states.)

The State Bureaucracy

It takes a lot of people to run the programs of state governments. These programs are carried out by several state departments called the state **bureaucracy.**

The people who run these state departments are called **bureaucrats.** Departments in state bureaucracies are sometimes called **boards** or **commissions.**

Some departments which most state bureaucracies include are:

- Board of Education
- Highway Department
- Health Department
- Public Utilities Commission
- Banking Commission
- Labor Board
- Environmental Protection Board
- Department of Public Safety
- Department of Public Assistance and Vocational Rehabilitation
- Department of Mental Health

The exact name of these departments may be different in each state, but the activities which the departments handle are the same.

Think About It

1. Who is the chief executive official in a state?
2. List five powers of state governors.
3. What does **plural executive** mean?
4. List the executive officials (titles) which are elected in your state.
5. Name one job which each of the following executive officials does:
   a. Lieutenant Governor
   b. Secretary of State
   c. Attorney General
   d. State Treasurer
6. What is the purpose of a state's bureaucracy?
7. Name five departments which most state bureaucracies have.

CHAPTER 23

The Executive Branch of the Federal Government

The **executive branch** is one of the three branches of the federal government. Its jobs are:

- to enforce federal laws;
- to carry on the day-to-day business of the federal government;
- to handle our country's relations with other countries.

The federal government has one **chief executive:** the **President.** There is also a **Vice President,** who becomes President if the President dies or resigns. Both serve 4-year terms.

Most of the work of carrying on the day-to-day business of the United States government is done by the **federal bureaucracy.**

Powers and Duties of the President

The U.S. Constitution gives the President the following powers and duties:

- See that the laws are carried out.
- Sign or veto bills which have been passed by Congress.
- Make treaties, but 2/3 of the Senate must **ratify** (approve) all treaties.
- Appoint ambassadors, Supreme Court Justices, and Cabinet members. The Senate must approve these appointments.

- If one of the officials appointed by the President leaves office while the Senate is not in session, the President may fill this vacancy without Senate approval until the Senate returns.
- Pardon someone who has been convicted of a federal crime, except for impeachment cases.
- Postpone or shorten the punishment of someone convicted of a federal crime. This is called granting a **reprieve.**
- Be commander-in-chief of the military. But remember, only Congress may declare war.
- Give Congress information about what is going on in the United States.

Suppose You Are President

Today is your first day on the job. You go to your office in the White House, called the **oval office** because of its shape. You walk around the room remembering how much history has been made here.

Then you look at your desk.

What is this huge stack of papers? You begin to read:

— The ambassador from Japan wants to talk about trade agreements.

— The ambassador from West Germany has some questions about military bases.

— Farmers in the midwest are angry about your budget proposals and want a meeting with you.

— You have been scheduled to speak in Baltimore tomorrow at a political party meeting.

— The Teachers' Association of North Carolina wants your support for a new education bill. They have sent you a copy of their reasons to read.

— The Chief of Naval Operations has just resigned. You must appoint another.

— The ambassador from an African republic wants to discuss foreign aid.

— Some citizens from California want your help in preserving a national forest.

You are not even near the bottom of the stack. **What will you do?**

Go on vacation?

Resign?

Get some help!

You can't go on vacation yet. The voters elected you to work.

Why resign? You spent millions of dollars getting elected.

So, get some help. Select a **staff**. Appoint a **Cabinet.**

The President's Staff

The President's **staff** helps with day-to-day work. The staff takes care of mail, sees visitors, answers the telephone, arranges the President's schedule, writes summaries of things the President needs to read. The President chooses members of the staff.

The President's Cabinet

The **Cabinet** is a group of official advisors to the President. The President appoints members of the Cabinet, but the Senate must approve all appointments. Each Cabinet member is head of one **executive department** of the **federal bureaucracy.**

Most Cabinet members have the title of **Secretary**. (The head law officer, the **Attorney General**, is the only one who does not.) The **Secretary of State** deals with foreign affairs. The **Secretary of the Treasury** deals with money. The **Secretary of the Interior** deals with public lands. The chart on the next page lists all 13 Cabinet members.

The Federal Bureaucracy

The President has many, many people to help run the programs of government. These people are organized into different **departments** of the executive branch. Together these departments are called the **federal bureaucracy.**

The federal bureaucracy is the hardest part of government to understand. It has more people than any other part of government. Almost three million people work in the federal bureaucracy. These people do many, many jobs. They deliver mail and coin money. Some inspect food. Others run federal prisons or investigate violations of federal laws. Still others protect national parks and wildlife. People who work in the federal bureaucracy are called **bureaucrats** or **civil servants.**

The federal bureaucracy has two parts. **Executive departments** are headed by Cabinet members. **Independent agencies** are not.

Executive Departments

Name of Department	Date Begun	Top Official
Department of **State**	1789	Secretary of State
Department of the **Treasury**	1789	Secretary of the Treasury
Department of **Defense**	1789	Secretary of Defense
Department of **Justice**	1870	Attorney General
Department of the **Interior**	1849	Secretary of the Interior
Department of **Agriculture**	1889	Secretary of Agriculture
Department of **Commerce**	1903	Secretary of Commerce
Department of **Labor**	1913	Secretary of Labor
Department of **Housing and Urban Development**	1965	Secretary of HUD
Department of **Transportation**	1966	Secretary of Transportation
Department of **Energy**	1977	Secretary of Energy
Department of **Education**	1979	Secretary of Education
Department of **Health and Human Services**	1979	Secretary of Health and Human Services

You will notice that the Department of Education and the Department of Health and Human Services are very new. The first executive department to handle education, health, and welfare was created in 1953. It was called the *Department of Health, Education, and Welfare.* In 1979 this department was split into two separate departments.

The top officials of all the executive departments are appointed by the President. Together they make up the President's **Cabinet.**

Each department head must be approved by the Senate. If the Senate does not approve a person appointed by the President, the President must appoint someone else. The President usually appoints close friends to these offices.

Most people who work in the executive departments are hired under a **merit system**. This means that anyone who wants a job in one of these departments must take a test. People with the highest scores on the test are hired first. This test is called the **civil service examination.**

Independent Agencies

Some jobs of the executive branch are done by people in **independent agencies.**

The two kinds of independent agencies are: independent **service** agencies and independent **regulatory** agencies.

110

Independent Service Agencies

> *Some independent agencies perform **services for the executive branch of the federal government.***

One of these independent service agencies gives merit tests for jobs in all of the executive departments. Another builds government buildings.

> *Some independent agencies perform **services for the people of the United States.***

The largest of these independent service agencies is the U.S. Postal Service. Another is the Veterans Administration. It runs hospitals and other programs for military veterans.

Independent Regulatory Agencies

Another kind of independent agency is the **independent regulatory agency.**

Independent regulatory agencies set standards for many products you buy and things you do. These standards, or **regulations**, must be obeyed just as laws must be obeyed.

Some examples of regulations made by independent regulatory agencies are:

- Labels on products you buy must tell the truth.
- Products you buy must meet safety standards.
- Sleepwear for babies and small children must meet fire safety standards.
- You must have a license to operate a CB radio.
- Nuclear power plants must meet safety standards.
- Airplanes, buses, and trains must meet safety standards.

The regulatory agencies of government should be fair to everyone. To make sure that these agencies cannot be controlled by any one person or political party, Congress made these rules:

- Each independent regulatory agency is headed by a group of 5-11 members called commissioners.
- The President appoints the commissioners, and they must be approved by the Senate.
- The commissioners serve long terms and are not all appointed at the same time. One President will probably not be in office long enough to appoint all the commissioners for any agency.

Keeping the regulatory agencies independent is one way that Congress makes sure the United States has a government of laws, not of people.

Checks and Balances

The Constitution created a **system of checks and balances** so that no branch of government would have too much power.

- Each branch has the power to **check** (stop) actions of the other branches.
- Each branch has powers which **balance** powers of the other branches.

**To keep the President
from having too much power:**

- The Senate must **ratify** (approve) all **treaties** made by the President.
- The Senate must approve all **appointments** made by the President.

- The Supreme Court may declare an action of the President to be unconstitutional.
- The House of Representatives may **impeach** (accuse) the President of a wrongdoing. The Senate may convict the President.
- Congress may **override** a veto.

To let the President check (stop) actions of the other two branches of government:

- The President may **veto** a bill passed by Congress.
- The President may **appoint** Justices of the Supreme Court.

Impeachment

Congress may remove a President, Vice President, or any executive official who commits a crime.

This is how it works:

- The House of Representatives must vote to **impeach** (officially accuse) the person.
- The Senate must then hold a trial to decide if the person who has been impeached (accused) is guilty.
- If the Senate decides (by a 2/3 vote) that the accused person is guilty, he or she must leave office.

Even if the person is convicted, the Senate cannot put the person in jail or give any other punishment except to remove the person from office.

The convicted person may be tried in a regular court and may be punished by the court. But this is **not** part of the impeachment-conviction process.

Only one President has ever been impeached. This was Andrew Johnson, the President who came after Abraham Lincoln. Johnson was impeached in 1868, but the Senate did not convict him.

Think About It

1. Name five powers and duties of the President.
2. Tell how the process of impeachment-conviction works.
3. Explain how the system of checks and balances works in the executive branch of the federal government.
4. What is the President's Cabinet?
5. What is the federal bureaucracy?
6. Name five executive departments of the federal government.
7. What is **merit hiring?**
8. Name one independent service agency.
9. List three ways that independent regulatory agencies protect people in the United States.
10. Explain what Congress has done to keep the regulatory agencies independent of political pressures so they can be fair to everyone.
11. Why do you think that the federal bureaucracy is the largest section of our government?

CHAPTER 24

Electing the President

President

Would you like to be President of the United States? A lot of people would!

How does a person get to be President?

Most Presidents get the job by being elected.

 A President is elected for a 4-year term.

A Vice President can also become President if the President dies or resigns. This has happened nine times in U.S. history. Eight times a President died and the Vice President became President. The most recent time was 1963. John Kennedy was assassinated, and Lyndon Johnson became President.

One time a President resigned. This was Richard Nixon. In 1974 Nixon was accused of a crime. When Nixon resigned, Vice President Gerald Ford became President.

Vice President

How does a person get to be Vice President?

Most Vice Presidents get the job by being elected along with the President for a 4-year term.

What happens if a Vice President dies or resigns? This happened in 1973. Spiro Agnew was Vice President then. He was accused of a crime, so he resigned. (Later, he was convicted of the crime.)

Did the United States have another election to pick a new Vice President?

No. The Constitution says that if a Vice President dies or resigns, the President may **nominate** a new Vice President.

Both houses of Congress must approve the new Vice President. If Congress does not approve, the President must choose someone else.

Giving Congress the power to approve the President's choice keeps the President from having too much power. The senators and representatives are elected by the voters. They speak for the voters when they vote on the President's choice of a new Vice President.

*Congress' power to approve the President's nomination is part of the **system of checks and balances.***

113

Ideas About Vice President

Different people have different ideas about how important a Vice President is.

Thomas Jefferson was Vice President from 1797 to 1801. He said that this "honorable and easy job" gave him "philosophical evenings in the winter and rural days in the summer."

John Nance Garner was Vice President from 1933 to 1941. Garner once said that the Vice Presidency wasn't worth "a pitcher of warm spit."

Hubert Humphrey had a different opinion of being Vice President. He served as Vice President from 1965 to 1969 while Lyndon Johnson was President. Humphrey had this to say about being Vice President:

> President Johnson saw fit to have me, as his Vice President, shoulder a share of his own burdens. I happily carried out the tasks he assigned to me—and, believe me, my winter evenings were seldom "philosophical," nor any summers "rural."
>
> Besides my constitutional duty to preside over the Senate . . . I held at least nine chairmanships on various national councils and was assigned as the President's liaison to local governments and to "plans for progress"—a minority employment effort. He sent me on foreign-policy missions abroad and on speech-making trips at home.
>
> Thomas Jefferson's notions of the Vice Presidency were accurate for his time. In those days, even the President didn't have much to do. Congress itself met a couple of months a year; and government in general occupied a secondary role compared to planting crops and expanding the frontiers and engaging in commerce and trade.

(Adapted from "The Vice Presidency," Los Angeles Times Service, San Antonio *Express*, February 21, 1973, p. 45.)

The Electoral College

Every four years the United States has a **presidential election**. This election is always in November. People who want to be President and Vice President campaign for many months before the election.

Election day arrives, and the voters cast their votes. This is called the **popular vote**. The team which gets the most votes in all the states wins. Right? Well, not always.

> The President and the Vice President are really chosen by **electors.**

What Is an Elector?

> **Electors** are people picked by the political parties in each state to vote for President and Vice President.

> All the electors together are called the **electoral college.**

How Many Electors Are There?

Each state has as many **electors** as it has senators and representatives.

Also, the District of Columbia has three **electors**. This makes a total of **538 electors.**

For Whom Do Electors Vote?

The **electors** are supposed to vote for the team which got the **most** popular votes in their state. Some states have a law that electors **must** vote for their state's winning team. In other states there is no such law. However, most of the time electors do vote the way they are supposed to.

What Does All of This Mean?

In every state, the winner of the **popular vote** (the vote of the people) gets **all** of that state's **electoral votes.**

The loser of the state's popular votes gets **no electoral votes.**

When all the votes from all of the states are counted, the winner of the popular vote could lose the election.

Sound confusing? Read on.

This Is What Happens on Election Day

- In every state, the voters go to the polls.

- At the voting booth, the ballot lists all the people running for President and Vice President. Candidates for the two offices run as a team.

- Each voter votes for a team for President and Vice President.

- Then the votes of the people are counted. This is called the popular vote.

- The candidate team with the most popular votes in each state wins all that state's electoral votes.

- The candidate team with the fewest votes in each state gets no electoral votes.

You are probably thinking that this system is not fair. A lot of people believe that this system is not fair.

What happened to the idea of one person, one vote?

Many people believe that the candidate team which wins the most votes from all the people in the United States should become the President and Vice President.

Let's look at the two main problems with the **electoral college** system.

Winner-Take-All Rule

The rule which says that **all** a state's **electoral votes** go to the winner of the **popular vote** is called the **winner-take-all** rule.

The sample election on the following page shows how the winner-take-all rule can cause the winner of the popular vote to lose the election.

Disproportionate Distribution of Electoral Votes

Another problem with the electoral college is the **disproportionate distribution of electoral votes**. This means that people in the United States are not equally represented in the electoral college.

The reason is the size of the electoral college and **how the electors are chosen**.

Each state has as many electors as it has representatives and senators in Congress

115

Representatives are divided among the states according to the population. Large states have many representatives. Smaller states have fewer representatives. Each representative speaks for about the same number of people. So the electors who are based on the number of each state's representatives are evenly divided among all the people in the United States. So far, this is <u>pro</u>portionate, not <u>dis</u>proportionate.

Each state has two senators. Large states have two senators. Small states have two senators. In the electoral college this means that both large and small states have two electoral votes for their two senators. The people in small states have a much greater voice in the electoral college than the people in large states. This is why we speak of a disproportionate distribution of electoral votes.

Two times in U.S. history, the loser of the **popular vote** received the most electoral votes and became President. This happened in 1876 (President Rutherford B. Hayes) and again in 1888 (President Benjamin Harrison).

In 1984, Ronald Reagan won 59% of the popular vote. But he won almost 98% of the electoral vote. A total of 525 of the 538 electoral votes went to Reagan. This made the election look very one-sided. However, 59% of the popular vote does not seem nearly so one-sided.

The **electoral vote** is not a true picture of the actual vote of the people. But, in fact, there is nothing in the Constitution that gives people the right to vote for President or the electors at all! State laws have given the people this right.

A Sample Election

	CANDIDATE 1		CANDIDATE 2	
	Popular Vote	Electoral Vote	Popular Vote	Electoral Vote
State A	26,000	5 + 2	24,000	0
State B	36,000	7 + 2	35,000	0
State C	45,000	0	65,000	11 + 2
Totals	107,000	16	124,000	13

Who Is the Real Winner?

Think About It

1. How do you suppose Candidate 1 in this sample election felt?
2. How do you suppose Candidate 2 in this sample selection felt?
3. How do you suppose the voters in State A and State B felt?
4. How do you suppose the voters in State C felt?
5. Do you believe the writers of the U.S. Constitution would have been happy with the results of this sample election? Why or why not?

Who Can Be President?

Do you still want to be President? Let's see if you qualify.

How old are you?

- If you are less than 35 years old, you are too young. You must wait a few years. The Constitution says that a person must be at least 35 years old to be President.

What else does the Constitution say?

- A President must be a *natural born* citizen of the United States. This means the President must be born in the United States or have parents who are U.S. citizens even if the President was not actually born in the United States.
- A President must have lived in the United States for 14 years.
- A President may only serve 10 years. Therefore, a person may only be elected two times. (Remember, a President's term is four years.) This rule allows a President to serve two full terms plus two years of the former President's term.

Example 1

—Mr. A is elected President in 1992.
—He serves one year and then he resigns.
—Mrs. B, the Vice President, serves the last three years of Mr. A's term.
—In 1996, Mrs. B is elected for a 4-year term.
—Can Mrs. B run a second time in the year 2000?

No. Mrs. B has already served seven years. Four more years would equal a total of 11 years. The Constitution says that one person may only serve 10 years as President.

Someone else will have to run for President in 2000.

Example 2

—Mrs. X is elected President in 1992.
—She serves two years. Then she dies.
—Mr. Y, the Vice President, becomes President and serves the last two years of Mrs. X's term.
—In 1996, Mr. Y is elected for a 4-year term.
—Can Mr. Y run a second time in the year 2000?

Yes. Because Mr. Y will have only served six years, he can run again in 2000.

> You can read about these rules in **Article 2, Section 1, and Amendment 22** of the U.S. Constitution.

Informal Requirements for President

Suppose you meet all the Constitution's requirements to be President. How likely are you to get elected?

Informal requirements for becoming President are not written in the Constitution. Informal requirements mean what most people look for in a President.

- Most people want a President who has political experience.
- A successful candidate must be a member of a major political party.
- A successful candidate must have a good personality, especially a good TV personality.

- A successful candidate must have good physical health and good emotional health.
- Most people would not vote for a candidate who was closely tied to big business, a labor union, or any other special interest group.
- So far, all of the U.S. Presidents have been white. Most have ancestors who came from Britain.
- All but one of our Presidents have been Protestant. John Kennedy was the first Catholic President. He was elected in 1960. No Jew has ever been President yet.
- No female has ever been President yet. Geraldine Ferraro was the first woman to run for Vice President. She ran in 1984.

Informal requirements change over time. An exception to an informal rule usually means that the candidate's other qualities are outstanding and outweigh this factor.

Think About It

1. Explain how a person becomes President in the United States.
2. What are two important problems with the electoral college system?
3. Name four informal requirements for President.

Can the United States Have a President Who Was Not Elected?

Most Presidents are elected to be President. Some Presidents have been elected to be Vice President and then taken the office of President when the President died. Once, however, the United States had a President who was not elected to either office. This is how it happened.

- The voters elected Richard Nixon to be President. Spiro Agnew was elected Vice President.

- Spiro Agnew resigned as Vice President because he was accused of a crime.

- President Nixon nominated Gerald Ford to be Vice President. Congress approved Ford as Vice President.

- The next year, Nixon was accused of a crime. The House of Representatives was ready to impeach (formally accuse) Nixon when Nixon resigned as President.

- Vice President Ford became President. **Ford was the first President who was not elected either President or Vice President by the voters.**

- President Ford nominated Nelson Rockefeller to be Vice President.

- Congress approved Rockefeller as Vice President.

Neither President Ford nor Vice President Rockefeller was elected to his office.

UNIT E SUMMARY

The executive branch at all levels of government enforces laws and carries out the day-to-day business of governments.

- The chief executive official in most cities is the **mayor.**

- The executive officials in counties are the county **commissioners** or **supervisors.**

- The chief executive official in state government is the **governor.**

- The chief executive official in the federal government is the **President.**

Executive officials of local and state governments are elected by the voters.

The President and Vice President of the United States are elected by an electoral college. The electors of the electoral college get their instructions from the popular vote, but the one person, one vote rule does not apply. The winner-take-all rule and the disproportionate distribution of electoral votes are two major problems with the electoral college.

The system of checks and balances works in the executive branch to keep executive officials from having too much power. The executive branch can also check (stop) actions of the other two branches so that no branch can have too much power.

Many jobs of the executive branch are done by bureaucrats—people who work in the executive departments and independent agencies. These bureaucrats are not elected. They must take a test to get their jobs.

UNIT E QUIZ

*Decide whether each statement below is **true** or **false**. Write **T** or **F** on your own paper. Then write a sentence which tells **why** each false statement is false.*

____ 1. Dividing the powers of government among three different branches is called the separation of powers.

____ 2. The executive branch of government makes the laws.

____ 3. A mayor is the chief executive officer of many counties.

____ 4. Most of the work of running cities is done by city departments.

____ 5. County commissioners are appointed by the governor of each state.

____ 6. County officials enforce state laws.

____ 7. The chief executive officer of each state is the governor.

____ 8. A plural executive system creates unity in the executive branch of state governments.

____ 9. Most of the day-to-day business of state government is done by the state bureaucracy.

____ 10. The chief executive officer of the federal government is the President.

____ 11. The only way to become President is to be elected to the office.

____ 12. If a Vice President dies or resigns, an election must be held to choose a new Vice President.

____ 13. The office of Vice President has always been a very busy and difficult job.

____ 14. Candidates for President run in a general election every four years.

____ 15. The candidate with the most popular votes in the general election always becomes President.

____ 16. There are 538 electors in the electoral college.

____ 17. The winner of a state's popular vote gets all of that state's electoral votes.

___18. All states have the same number of electors.

___19. The President must be at least 35 years old.

___20. The President must be a natural-born citizen of the United States.

___21. The Constitution says that a President may serve only eight years.

___22. Informal requirements for President change over time as voters' attitudes change.

___23. The President may veto bills passed by Congress.

___24. The President may make treaties with foreign countries.

___25. A President or Vice President may be removed from office by being impeached by the House of Representatives and convicted by the Senate.

___26. Each branch of government has the power to stop actions of the other branches.

___27. Congress may override a President's veto.

___28. Members of the President's Cabinet must be elected.

___29. Most people who work in the executive departments of the federal government are appointed to their jobs by the President.

___30. Independent regulatory agencies in the federal bureaucracy help to control the safety of many consumer products.

Learning Objectives for Unit F

When you have finished this lesson, you will be able to:

- Name the main officials in the judicial system.

- Explain the function of trial courts and appellate courts.

- Explain the function of a petit jury and a grand jury.

- Recognize the plaintiff and the defendant in a court case.

- Explain the difference between civil and criminal cases.

- Recognize cases which would be tried in federal courts.

- Tell what cases the U.S. Supreme Court may decide to hear.

- Tell what cases the U.S. Supreme Court must hear.

- Explain the main function of the U.S. Supreme Court.

- Understand how decisions of the Supreme Court influence U.S. government.

- Explain how the system of checks and balances works in the judicial branch.

- Explain due process of law and list the rights of a defendant.

- List the rights of a plaintiff in a court case.

UNIT F

THE JUDICIAL BRANCH OF GOVERNMENT

The third branch of government is called the **judicial branch.**

The judicial branch
- decides what the law means and
- settles problems that people have with the law.

In this unit you will learn about the judicial branches of local, state, and federal governments.

SUPREME COURT JUSTICES
The Supreme Court is the highest court in the land. It has 9 Justices. They are appointed by the President, but their appointments must be approved by the Senate.

Two Court Systems

Legal questions and conflicts are settled in courts of law. The judicial branch has two sets of courts: **state courts** and **federal courts.**

State courts handle most of the court cases in the United States. They serve local areas as well as their whole state.

Federal courts handle cases which involve

- federal laws or treaties,
- the federal government, or
- more than one state.

Officers of the Court

Judges are the main officials in the judicial branch.

Each court has at least one judge. Some courts have more than one judge. Some judges are elected by the voters; other judges are appointed by the governor (for state courts) or by the President (for federal courts).

The **court clerk** is another important official in the judicial branch. The court clerk

- keeps court records,
- arranges the court schedule, and
- collects fees and fines.

Plaintiff and Defendant

Every court case has two sides. One side accuses the other side of some wrongdoing. Each side may be either a person or a group.

Plaintiff

> The **plaintiff** is the person or group who takes the case to court.

Defendant

> The **defendant** is the person or group who is accused of doing something wrong.

In a court case, the **plaintiff** accuses the **defendant** of doing something wrong. The plaintiff asks the court to correct the wrong done by the defendant or to punish the defendant for the wrong act.

In every court case, both the **plaintiff** and the **defendant** may

- tell their side,
- have witnesses for their side,
- ask the other side questions,
- have a lawyer to help them.

Your Rights as a Defendant: Due Process of Law

If you are arrested, you have these rights:

- to be told what crime you are accused of;
- not to answer questions;
- to have a lawyer with you when the police question you;
- not to pay unreasonable bail;
- to have a public trial;
- to have a jury which is not biased against you;
- to have a judge who is not biased against you;
- to have a lawyer defend you at your trial;
- to have witnesses speak for you at your trial;
- not to be a witness against yourself;
- to see and hear the witnesses against you;
- to ask questions of the other side;
- not to be tried more than once for the same crime.

These rights are called **due process of law**. These rights were written into the U.S. Constitution to protect innocent people who are falsely accused of a crime.

Your Rights as a Plaintiff

If someone commits a crime against you, you have these rights:

- to have the police, sheriff, or FBI find and arrest the guilty person;
- to have the government act as plaintiff for you (represent you) at the trial;
- to have a public trial;
- to have a jury which is not biased against you;
- to have a judge who is not biased against you;
- to have witnesses speak for you at the trial;
- to ask questions of the other side at the trial.

You may read about these rights in the U.S. Constitution, **Amendments 5, 6, and 8 of the Bill of Rights.**

Think About It

1. Name the main officers of the judicial branch of government.
2. Explain who the plaintiff in a court case is and what rights the plaintiff has.
3. Explain who the defendant in a court case is and what rights the defendant has.

Civil Cases

 Civil cases are ***disputes about people's legal rights.***

Example 1

Mike buys your old motorcycle. He signs a contract to pay you $50 a month.

Three months later, Mike wrecks the motorcycle. He also stops paying you.

Because Mike signed a contract with you, you have a legal right to be paid the full amount Mike owes you, even though the motorcycle is wrecked.

You may take Mike to court. If the court agrees with you that your contract was correctly written, the court will order Mike to finish paying you what he owes you.

In this case, you are the **plaintiff**. Mike is the **defendant.**

Example 2

You and your band are playing at a party in a big, old barn. Suddenly the roof caves in. Three of the band's instruments are ruined, and two of you have broken arms. Another band member has bad cuts and bruises.

The owner of the barn refuses to pay for the repairs to your instruments or for your medical expenses. You take him to court.

You believe the owner of the barn is responsible for your damage and injuries because he neglected to repair his barn.

If the court agrees with you, the court will order the owner to pay the costs for repairing your instruments and also the costs of your medical care.

In this case, your band is the **plaintiff**. The owner of the barn is the **defendant.**

*The court's decision in a civil case is called a **judgment.***

Criminal Cases

Criminal cases decide
- whether a person has broken a criminal law and
- what the punishment should be.

Crimes are actions against society. Because of this, the government is always the plaintiff in a criminal case. The government lawyer in a criminal case is called the **prosecutor** or the **prosecution**. The defendant is the person or group accused of the crime.

There are two kinds of criminal actions: **felonies** and **misdemeanors.**

A **felony** is a major crime. Murder, rape, armed robbery, kidnapping, and arson are felonies.

A **misdemeanor** is a minor crime. Vagrancy, simple assault, and trespassing are misdemeanors.

*The court's decision in a criminal case is called the **verdict.***

Think About It

1. Explain the difference between civil and criminal court cases.
2. What is the difference between a felony and a misdemeanor?
3. What is the difference between a judgment and a verdict?

Trial Courts

Both the state court system and the federal court system have two kinds of courts: trial courts and appeals courts.

Trial courts do two things:
- hear the evidence about a case and
- make a decision about the case.

In trial courts, a case may be heard by a judge and a jury, or a case may be heard by a judge alone. In some cases, this choice is made by the people involved in the case.

The U.S. Constitution says that **all** federal criminal cases **must** have a jury trial.

The trial court's decision in a civil case is called a **judgment**. The court's decision in a criminal case is called the **verdict.**

Petit Jury

The jury in a trial court is called a **petit jury**. In federal trial courts, the petit jury has 12 members. In state trial courts, the petit jury has either six or 12 members.

Grand Jury

You have already learned about the **grand jury**. The grand jury is not a trial jury. The grand jury hears evidence about a case to decide if the case should go to trial. If the grand jury believes that there is enough evidence, the case goes to trial. But the grand jury doesn't decide who wins the case. That is the job of the petit jury.

Appeals Courts

Appeals courts hear cases which have already been tried in a **trial court.**

A case which has been tried in a trial court may be appealed to an appeals court if the original trial was unfair or if new evidence is found. The appeals court may **reverse** (change) or **uphold** (keep) the decision of the trial court.

Appeals courts do not have juries, and they do not hear witnesses. Judges in appeals courts read the record of the first trial. They also listen to what the lawyers for both sides have to say about why the trial court's decision should be changed.

In a criminal case, the defendant may appeal the trial court's **verdict** to a higher court.

In a civil case, either side may appeal the trial court's **judgment** to a higher court.

Think About It

1. Explain what the jobs of trial courts and appeals courts are.
2. Explain the difference between a petit jury and a grand jury.

129

CHAPTER 26

State Courts

Each state has a system of courts. The courts in all the states are very much alike, even though the names of the courts may be different. Most court cases in the United States are handled in the state court system.

State Judges

Most judges in state courts are elected by the voters. Some state judges are appointed by the state's governor. A few state judges are elected by their state legislature.

Three Levels of Courts

Each state's court system is different. However, each state has three levels of courts: **local courts, county courts,** and **appeals courts.**

Local Courts

Local courts are the first level of courts in a state's judicial system.

Local courts handle cases which involve city or county ordinances or state laws.

Some local courts which many states have are:

Justice of the Peace—sometimes called the **JP court.** The justice of the peace is a judge, although he or she doesn't have to have any legal education. JPs are elected by the people in their area. JPs perform marriages and handle minor problems. A charge of drunkenness, a family fight, or a bounced check would be handled by a JP.

City courts—sometimes called **police courts** or **municipal courts.** City courts handle traffic cases and other cases involving city ordinances.

Small claims courts—handle civil cases involving a small amount of money.

County Courts (Trial Courts)

County courts—sometimes called **superior courts** or **district courts**—are the main **trial** courts in the state judicial system.

Some county courts specialize in one area of the law such as:

Juvenile courts—typical case: a person under the age of 18 is accused of breaking a state law.

Family courts—typical cases: divorce, child abuse, child custody.

Many state trial courts have **original jurisdiction** (they hear a case for the first time) and also hear appeals from lower courts. State trial courts handle **civil** and **criminal** cases.

Appeals Courts

Every state has at least one top state court. Cases may be appealed to this court from all the lower courts.

Some states have separate top appeals courts for civil and criminal cases.

In many states, the highest appeals court is called the **state supreme court.**

Think About It

1. How do judges in state courts get these jobs?
2. Which court system handles most of the court cases in the United States?
3. What are the three levels of state courts? Name some kinds of cases handled by each level of court.

COUNTY COURTROOM (Trial Court)
The U.S. Constitution guarantees every citizen the right to a trial by jury. Think back to Chapter 14. Why is this right so important?

CHAPTER 27

Federal Courts

The U.S. Constitution created a **Supreme Court** and gave Congress the power to create whatever lower courts are needed.

Today, the **federal court system** includes

U.S. District Courts (trial courts),
U.S. Courts Of Appeal, and the
U.S. Supreme Court.

The U.S. Constitution gave Congress the power to create both federal trial courts and federal courts of appeal.

Federal Judges

All judges of federal courts are appointed by the President and must be approved by the U.S. Senate.

Judges of most federal courts are appointed for life. They cannot be removed from office except by impeachment and conviction.

Judges of a few of the lower courts are appointed for a certain number of years.

Federal Trial Courts

U.S. District Courts are the **trial** courts in the federal court system. Most federal cases start in U.S. District Courts. The United States has 90 District Courts.

You have already learned that most court cases in the United States are handled in state courts.

Some cases which are handled in U.S. District Courts are:

- A person accused of breaking a federal law is tried in a U.S. District Court.
- A disagreement between two states is decided in a U.S. District Court.
- A disagreement between a state and the federal government is decided in a U.S. District Court.
- A disagreement between two people from different states may be handled in a U.S. District Court, or the people involved may go to a state court. It is their choice.

ANY case which involves a federal law, a federal treaty, or has anything to do with the U.S. Constitution may be taken to a federal court.

Federal Appeals Courts

U.S. Courts Of Appeals (sometimes called **U.S. Circuit Courts Of Appeals**) handle appeals from U.S. District Courts.

The United States has 11 Circuit Courts of Appeals.

U.S. Supreme Court

The **U.S. Supreme Court** is the highest court in the United States.

Justices of the U.S. Supreme Court

The U.S. Supreme Court has nine judges who are called **Justices.**

Justices of the U.S. Supreme Court are appointed by the President, approved by the Senate, and serve for life. They may be removed from office only by impeachment and conviction.

What Cases Does the U.S. Supreme Court Hear?

Supreme Court cases fall into two different groups: cases which start in the Supreme Court (original jurisdiction) and cases which come to the Supreme Court **on appeal** (appellate jurisdiction).

Original Jurisdiction

Original jurisdiction means that a court may hear a case for the first time.

A few kinds of cases might start in the U.S. Supreme Court.

A case **between two states** or a case **between the federal government and a state** could begin in the U.S. Supreme Court. Most such cases usually begin in a U.S. District Court, however.

Cases on Appeal

Almost all cases which come before the U.S. Supreme Court are **appealed** from a lower court. These cases are said to come **on appeal.**

Many cases are appealed to the U.S. Supreme Court every year. The Supreme Court must **consider** every case which comes to it on appeal. In some of these cases, it will agree to **hear** the case—that is, to make a formal, full-scale decision about it. But the Supreme Court doesn't have to hear all of the cases it considers. It actually hears only a few of them.

The Supreme Court **must** hear some cases.

- If the highest court in a state upholds a **state law**, and there is good reason to believe that this state law violates a federal law or treaty or goes against the U.S. Constitution, the U.S. Supreme Court **must** hear the case.
- If the highest court in a state declares a **federal law or treaty** unconstitutional, the U.S. Supreme Court **must** hear the case.

For all other cases which are appealed to the U.S. Supreme Court, the Supreme Court Justices decide if the case is important enough for the Court to hear.

The U.S. Supreme Court **only** hears cases which will **affect a large group of people.**

The actual case might involve only one person or a few people, but the **issue involved** must affect a large number of people.

133

How Do Cases Get to the U.S. Supreme Court?

A case may reach the U.S. Supreme Court in two ways:

- Cases may come from **state courts**. Such a case must first
  - go through all the state courts of appeals and
  - be heard by the highest court in that state.

    Then the case may be appealed to the U.S. Supreme Court.
- Cases may start in any **federal trial court**. These cases must then
  - be heard by a U.S. Circuit Court of Appeals.

    Then the case may be appealed to the U.S. Supreme Court.

What Is the Main Job of the U.S. Supreme Court?

The **main job** of the U.S. Supreme Court is to **decide what the law means.**

Many times a law which is passed by Congress is written in general terms. Everyone may not agree about what the law says or what the law means.

You have learned that the U.S. Constitution is a general plan for government. Everyone does not always agree about what the Constitution means.

When people disagree about the meaning of a law or the meaning of some part of the U.S. Constitution, the U.S. Supreme Court decides exactly what the law or the Constitution means.

Questions about the law and the Constitution are often very difficult to answer. Sometimes not even the justices on the Supreme Court can agree. When this happens, the decision of the majority of the justices is the decision of the Court.

Real Cases

No matter how unfair or bad a law is or how much people disagree about the meaning of a law, the Supreme Court cannot rule on the law unless a **real case** is brought to the Court.

A **real case** means that someone must actually break a law or show that a law directly affects him or her. The case must then be brought to court.

The rule about real cases is part of the system of **separation of powers**. This rule makes sure that the legislative branch and the judicial branch of government are separate from each other and can make independent decisions.

Judges cannot give opinions about laws which Congress is thinking about passing. Judges cannot even give opinions about a law which Congress has already passed until the law is challenged in a **real case**.

Courts can **only** make decisions in **r**eal cases which **are brought to trial.**

An Issue of Free Speech

The people of Yourtown have just learned that Company X is dumping radioactive waste in fields and open ditches in Yourtown. Many people in Yourtown are very angry.

You and a small group of other people organize a protest demonstration in front of Company X's main offices.

The president of Company X calls the police who come and arrest you and the other demonstrators. You are all charged with having a demonstration without a permit. Five people in the group are charged with trespassing on Company X's property.

The case is taken to a trial court in your state, and everyone in your group is found guilty.

You appeal the case to your state's highest court of appeals. The trial court's decision is upheld. You are all very disappointed because you believe your right of free speech has been denied. Free speech is guaranteed in the Bill of Rights.

You decide to appeal your case to the U.S. Supreme Court.

- You know that the Supreme Court gets many more appeals than it actually hears.
- You know that the Supreme Court only hears cases which affect a lot of people.
- You also know that the U.S. Constitution guarantees everyone the right to free speech.

The Justices of the U.S. Supreme Court decide that your case is important enough for them to hear. They must decide just exactly what the right to free speech means.

If you were a Justice of the U.S. Supreme Court, how would you vote?

Think About It

1. How do federal court judges get their jobs?
2. What is the term of office for most federal court judges?
3. What kinds of cases are handled by federal trial courts?
4. How do most cases get to the U.S. Supreme Court?
5. What is the main job of the U.S. Supreme Court?
6. What is a *real* case?

CHAPTER 28 *Supreme Court Decisions*

You have just learned that the main job of the U.S. Supreme Court is to decide what the Constitution and the law mean.

When people disagree about what the Constitution means or about what a law means, and when a real case is brought to court, the highest court in which the question can be settled is the Supreme Court.

Every year the Supreme Court hears many important cases. Every year the Supreme Court makes important decisions about the rights and liberties of U.S. citizens.

Some of the most important Supreme Court decisions have dealt with the rights which are guaranteed to all U.S. citizens by the Bill of Rights and by the other amendments to the Constitution. You studied the Bill of Rights and the amendments in Unit C.

Here are four examples of Supreme Court decisions which protect your rights as a U.S. citizen.

- In the first example, the Supreme Court protected your right to **religious freedom.**
- In the second example, the Supreme Court protected your right **to be treated equally by the laws** no matter what color of skin you have.
- The third example is a Supreme Court decision which makes sure that **your vote is equal to everyone else's** when choosing members of the U.S. House of Representatives and members of state legislatures.
- Example four is a Supreme Court decision which protects **your rights if you are arrested.**

Freedom of Religion

Many of the early settlers came to America to find religious freedom. In England, the church and the state were not separate. The government supported an official church. Everyone's tax money supported this official church. Everyone had to follow the rules of this official church. The people were not free to choose their own religion.

The Bill of Rights guarantees all U.S. citizens the freedom to choose their own religion.

- The government may not get involved in any religion.
- The government may not favor one religion over others.
- The government may not use the people's tax money to support any religion.

In the early 1960s two cases about religious freedom in public schools were appealed to the Supreme Court. One case was about prayers in public schools. The other case was about reading Bible verses in public schools.

The Supreme Court ruled that having prayers or reading Bible verses in public schools **violated the separation of church and state.**

Every school child and every family has the right to pray the way they wish—or not to pray at all. Every school child and every family has the right to read the Bible or not read the Bible. A public school does **not** have the right to say to public school children, "now we will pray," or "now we will all read the Bible." These are private matters for each individual and family to decide for themselves.

The Supreme Court's decision in these cases protected your right to

- choose your own religion—or choose no religion,
- choose how you want to practice your own religious beliefs, and
- not have your tax money used to support any religion.

Equal Protection of the Laws

Amendment 14 to the U.S. Constitution guarantees **equal protection of the laws** to all U.S. citizens. This means that laws must be applied equally to all people.

The 1954 Supreme Court case of **Brown v. Board of Education of Topeka** was about equal protection of the laws.

Mr. Brown had sued the public schools of Topeka, Kansas. The Topeka school district would not let Mr. Brown's 8-year-old daughter, Linda, go to the all-white school near her home because she was black. Mr. Brown said that the law should treat his daughter the same as all the other children in the neighborhood, no matter if she was black or white.

Mr. Brown lost his case in the Kansas state courts. He appealed the case to the U.S. Supreme Court.

The Supreme Court agreed to hear this case because the issue was important to a large group of people.

All of the Justices on the Supreme Court agreed with Mr. Brown. They ruled that **segregated** schools were not equal. A law which made children go to a separate school just because of the color of their skin denied these children equal protection of the laws. This was a violation of Amendment 14 to the U.S. Constitution.

The Supreme Court ordered all public schools to be **desegregated** "with all deliberate speed." "All deliberate speed" means that the schools should begin to make plans and move as quickly as possible to desegregate.

Not all schools have moved as quickly as possible to end segregation. However, the Supreme Court's ruling in **Brown v. Board of Education of Topeka** was a very important step toward ending segregation.

One Person, One Vote

Members of state legislatures are elected from **election districts** in their states. The first election districts in many states were the same as counties. Most counties in a state are about the same geographical size. Each election district, or county, had the same number of members in the state legislature, no matter how many people lived in that district.

This system worked fairly well as long as the population of the states was spread fairly evenly over the state. However, as more of the U.S. population moved to cities, counties, and thus election districts, became very different in population size. Legislators from cities represented many people. Legislators from rural counties represented fewer people.

Voters in cities believed that this system was not fair. It did not follow the one person, one vote idea of a representative government.

In the case of **Reynolds v. Sims**, the U.S. Supreme Court ruled that election districts for choosing members of state legislatures must be based on population, not geographical area. The Supreme Court said that "legislators represent people, not trees or acres." Voting districts must be as equal in population size as possible.

This decision makes sure that everyone's vote is equal to everyone else's.

Rights of Accused People

The Constitution guarantees that people accused of crimes do not have to give evidence against themselves. It also says accused persons have the right to have a lawyer to help them.

Many people do not know about their Constitutional rights. Many people be-come frightened if they are arrested and might forget about their rights. Sometimes police officers may try to force a person to admit that he or she is guilty. Also, some people cannot afford a lawyer.

No matter what rights are guaranteed in the Constitution, if people do not know their rights, these rights will not do them much good.

In the case of **Miranda v. Arizona**, the U.S. Supreme Court ruled that when a person is arrested, the police must tell the person what rights he or she has.

You have probably heard people speak of the police reading suspects their "Miranda rights." This expression comes from the **Miranda v. Arizona** case.

The rights referred to are those which are guaranteed in the Bill of Rights. These rights include

- the right to remain silent when you are arrested,
- the right to have a lawyer present when you are questioned,
- the right to have a lawyer appointed to represent you, even if you cannot afford to pay the lawyer.

Think About It

1. How have Supreme Court decisions protected the freedom of religion?
2. What issue did *Brown v. Board of Ed. of Topeka* deal with?
3. How did the Supreme Court make sure that everyone's vote is equal to everyone else's?
4. What rights did *Miranda v. Arizona* protect?

CHAPTER 29

Checks and Balances in the Judicial Branch

The writers of the U.S. Constitution didn't want any one branch of government to become too powerful. So they created a **system of checks and balances** which applies to all three branches of the federal government.

To let the judicial branch check the other two branches of government:

> The judicial branch makes sure the executive branch **prosecutes cases fairly.**

The **prosecutor** in criminal cases is always the government. (The prosecutor is the person who brings a criminal case to court.)

Because it is the executive branch's job to enforce the law, a member of the Justice Department speaks for the government. (The Justice Department is one of the executive departments.)

It is the prosecutor's job to prove that the defendant is guilty. But it is the job of the federal court to be sure that the prosecutor has a true case against the defendant. The court also makes sure that the prosecutor treats the defendant fairly.

The federal courts decide whether a law passed by Congress or a state legislature is constitutional—that is, whether the law agrees with the Constitution or goes against the Constitution.

However, the courts may only rule on a law after a **real case** is brought to court.

> The federal courts decide if an **action** of the President or any executive agency is **constitutional.**

However, no court may say anything about any action of the executive branch until a **real case** is brought to trial.

Congress can act as a check on the power of federal courts in two ways:

- The House of Representatives can **impeach** a federal judge and the Senate can **convict** the federal judge.
- Congress can **amend** the U.S. Constitution.

To balance power between the three branches of the federal government:

- the President **appoints federal judges**, but the Senate must **approve** these appointments.

Checks and Balances
The Three Branches of Government

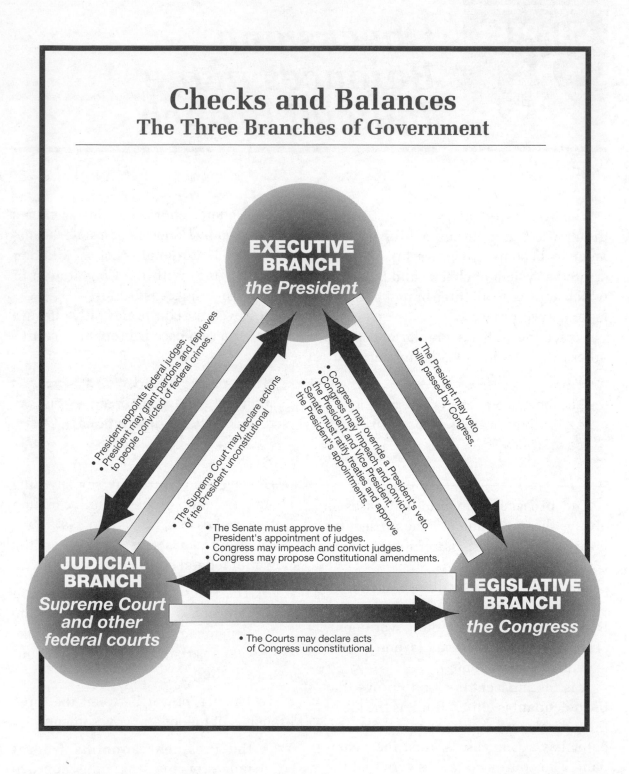

EXECUTIVE
BRANCH
the President

JUDICIAL
BRANCH
*Supreme Court
and other
federal courts*

LEGISLATIVE
BRANCH
the Congress

• President appoints federal judges.
• President may grant pardons and reprieves to people convicted of federal crimes.

• The Supreme Court may declare actions of the President unconstitutional.

• Congress may override a President's veto.
• Congress may impeach and convict the President and Vice President.
• Senate must ratify treaties and approve President's appointments.

• The President may veto bills passed by Congress.

• The Senate must approve the President's appointment of judges.
• Congress may impeach and convict judges.
• Congress may propose Constitutional amendments.

• The Courts may declare acts of Congress unconstitutional.

UNIT F SUMMARY

The Judicial Branch of government decides what laws mean and settles problems which people have with the law.

The United States has two sets of courts—state courts and federal courts. Each court has at least one judge. Some courts have more than one judge.

The person or group who takes a case to court is called the plaintiff. The person or group who is accused of doing something wrong is called the defendant.

The U.S. Constitution protects the rights of both the plaintiff and the defendant.

The U.S. Supreme Court is the highest court in the judicial system. It has the final say in disagreements about what the Constitution or other laws mean. Many times in the history of our government the Supreme Court has made a decision which has had a great influence on many people.

The judicial branch, and especially the Supreme Court, is the guardian of our freedom.

The chart on the previous page summarizes the system of checks and balances. Notice how each branch has ways to check (stop) actions of the other branches.

UNIT F QUIZ

*Decide whether each statement below is **true** or **false**. Write **T** or **F** on your own paper. Then write a sentence which tells **why** each false statement is false.*

___ 1. Most court cases in the United States are handled by federal courts.

___ 2. Judges are the major officials in the judicial branch of government.

___ 3. A plaintiff is the person who is accused of a crime.

___ 4. In a court case, both the plaintiff and the defendant have the right to tell their side of the case.

___ 5. If you are arrested, you have the right to know what crime you are accused of.

___ 6. If you are charged with a crime, the police or the judge may decide to hold your trial in secret.

___ 7. If you are accused of a crime, you must tell the judge and the jury what you did wrong.

___ 8. If you are accused of a crime, you have the right to see and hear the witnesses against you.

___ 9. If you are the victim of a crime, you have the right to have the government represent you at the trial of the person accused of the crime.

___10. Only the defendant has the right to bring witnesses to the trial.

___11. A civil case decides if a person has committed a crime.

___12. The court's decision in a civil case is called a judgment.

___13. A misdemeanor is a major crime.

___14. The court's decision in a criminal case is called the verdict.

___15. An appeals court is the first court to hear the evidence and make a decision about a case.

___16. A petit jury is a trial jury.

___17. A grand jury decides if the defendant is guilty or not guilty.

___18. An appeals court usually has a jury.

142

___19. The Constitution requires that all federal criminal cases must have jury trials.

___20. Justices of the Peace handle minor problems.

___21. State trial courts hear cases involving state laws.

___22. An appeals court may reverse or uphold the decision of the trial court.

___23. Most federal judges are elected.

24. Federal courts handle cases involving the U.S. Constitution or a federal law or treaty.

___25. The U.S. Supreme Court is the highest court in the United States.

___26. Most cases heard by the U.S. Supreme Court begin in the Supreme Court.

___27. The main job of the U.S. Supreme Court is to decide what the law means.

___28. The Supreme Court cannot give an opinion about a law unless a real case involving the law is brought to court.

___29. Over the years, many Supreme Court decisions have protected the rights of U.S. citizens.

___30. Judges may be removed from office by impeachment and conviction.

Learning Objectives for Unit G

When you have finished this unit, you will be able to:

- Tell who can vote in the United States.

- Explain how a person registers to vote in the United States.

- Explain the importance of the secret ballot.

- Explain what lobbying means and who can lobby.

- Tell what a primary election is and what a general election is.

- Explain the two different ways that states choose candidates for President.

- Name the two major political parties in the United States.

- Explain the importance of minor political parties in the United States.

- Explain who pays the costs of running governments.

- Tell how government funds are spent at the local, state, and federal levels.

- Explain how citizens can have a say in how government money is spent.

- Understand some of the important influences on people's political beliefs.

UNIT G

THE PEOPLE AND THE GOVERNMENT

You would probably agree that people need laws and government, and that good laws and government protect the rights of the people.

 *Laws and government should be **for the people.***

The writers of the U.S. Constitution believed that laws and government should be for the people. Most of the leaders of the government in the United States today believe this. But how can we be sure that our laws and our governments really do protect our rights?

The best way to be sure that laws and government really do protect your rights is to get involved in government.

You have learned what the Congress and the state legislatures do in our government.

You have learned what the President and the executive departments, the mayors and city council members, the county and state officials do in our government.

You have learned what the judges of the courts do in our government.

But what can the people do?
The answer: a lot.

In a representative democracy, the people have a lot of power.

In this unit you will learn what you and other U.S. citizens can do to make sure that your laws and your government protect your rights and your freedoms. You will also learn about political parties, how the two major political parties began, and the importance of minor political parties.

This unit explains who pays the costs of governments and how you as a citizen can have a say in how your governments spend their money.

This unit also talks about various influences on people's political beliefs.

CHAPTER 30

Influencing Your Government

Voting

The main way that most people can have a say in government is by **voting.**

The U.S. Constitution makes some rules about who can vote in every state.

> All states **must** follow the rules which are stated in the U.S. Constitution.

The U.S. Constitution says:

> No state may deny a person the right to vote because of **race, color, sex,** or **age**, if the person is 18 years old or over.

You may read these rules in **Amendments 15, 19,** and **26** in the U.S. Constitution.

All U.S. citizens who are 18 years of age or older may vote, both men and women of any race or color. The only people who cannot vote are those who have lost their rights of citizenship because they are legally judged to be mentally incompetent or have been convicted of a serious crime.

A History of Voting Rights

When the U.S. Constitution was first written, only white men over the age of 21 could vote. In some cases, only adult white men who owned property could vote.

- In **1870 black men** were given the right to vote by **Amendment 15** to the U.S. Constitution.
- In **1920** all **women** were given the right to vote by **Amendment 19** to the U.S. Constitution.
- In **1971** all U.S. citizens **18 years old and older** were given the right to vote by **Amendment 26** to the U.S. Constitution.

How Do You Vote?

Suppose this is the year for a presidential election.

Today is October 1, and the general election is Tuesday, November 5. That's only 35 days from now!

In just three weeks you'll be 18. This will be your first vote, and you're very excited.

You've been following the campaigns for several months, and you've made up your mind how you will vote.

In today's newspaper your read a notice: "Only five more days to register to vote!" Five days? You won't be 18 for three more weeks! What will you do?

You phone the voter registration office at the county courthouse.

"Yes, you must register at least 30 days

before the election in this state," the clerk tells you. "It takes us 30 days to get the voter lists ready."

"We must have voter lists to be sure everyone who comes to vote really lives in this district," the clerk continues.

"We also must be sure that no one votes more than one time in each election. But you may register as much as 30 days before you turn 18," the clerk adds.

"All right!" you say with relief. "For a minute there, I was a bit worried."

Whew! The law is on your side.

"How do I register?" you ask the clerk.

"Well, you may come down to this office and fill out a registration form," she tells you.

"But if you prefer, you may just fill out the form which is printed in the newspaper and mail that form to us. There's still time. Or, your high school should have some forms in their office. Or you could get a form from any post office."

"Just get a form, fill it out, and mail it today. We'll take care of the rest. Your voter registration card will be mailed to you. It should reach you in a couple of weeks."

Sure enough, two weeks later your voter registration card arrives in the mail. Not bad.

November 5 arrives. You decide to go vote before you go to your first class. The voting place for your district is the gym of your high school. Most voting places are in large public buildings.

You walk in and find a very long line. Some of your friends and a few teachers are standing there with a great many other people.

"Where do we vote?" you ask.

"Right here," they tell you.

"Is this the line?" You are surprised that the line is so long.

The line moves quickly. You notice a large number of voting booths all around the gym. There must be 30, maybe more.

If that many people can vote at one time, the line should move pretty fast, you decide. But, if it's a choice between standing in line here or going to math class, you're not sure you want the line to move too fast.

After a short chat with your friends, you find yourself at a long table. You notice several signs: "A-F," "G-L," "M-R," "S-Z." You go to the place for your initial.

The election helper at the table looks at your voter registration card and finds your name in the large book. Then she stamps **voted** by your name. "That must be the voter registration list," you decide.

Then you sign your name on a long paper and pick up a **ballot**—a piece of paper which lists all the people running for office.

You look at the voting booths. You know that in some places they contain special voting machines, but here they do not.

"Which voting booth do I go to?" you ask.

"Any empty one. It doesn't matter which one."

You go to an empty voting booth and mark your ballot. Simple as that.

Secret Ballot

A very important fact about voting in the United States is that all ballots are secret. No one but you, the voter, needs to know how you vote.

It hasn't always been that way. In fact, at one time many elections used a show of hands or a voice vote.

Sometimes the candidates were even watching and listening as people told how they wanted to vote.

Today, all states use the secret ballot in all elections. A federal law says that all federal elections must use a secret ballot.

Why is a secret ballot so important?

A secret ballot guarantees your right to vote the way you want to. If no one can see how you vote, no one can make you vote for a candidate you don't want. And no one can punish you for the way you voted.

Lobbying

Another way that people can have a say in what government officials do is to **lobby.**

 Lobbying is talking or writing to someone to influence his or her decision.

Suppose your government teacher plans to give a big test on Monday after your school's biggest game.

Everyone in your class is unhappy. So you and the other students get together and decide on a plan.

You choose two students who have good persuasive skills. These two students become the **lobbyists** for your class. They meet with your teacher and explain the class' point of view. They might even invite the teacher to lunch.

As lobbyists, the students hope to gain the good will of the teacher and persuade him or her to make a decision in their group's favor.

Many groups in the United States hire lobbyists to influence lawmakers and other government officials in local, state, and federal governments.

Government officials listen to what lobbyists have to say because the lobbyists represent voters. Government officials fig-

ure that if these voters care enough about an issue to hire a lobbyist, they care enough to vote on election day.

All lobbyists do not work for a group or an organization. Anyone can be a lobbyist, even you and your classmates.

In your town or county, you can talk directly with a government official. You can write letters to state and federal officials to tell them your views.

Choosing Candidates for Political Office

You have just voted in the general election. The ballot on which you marked your vote listed the **candidates** for every office.

 A candidate is a person who runs for an elected office.

How did these candidates get on the ballot? Who chose them to be candidates?

Primary Elections

Each political party chooses its own candidate for each office. Each party holds a **primary election** a few months before the **general election.**

A primary election is an election to choose a party's candidate for the general election.

Candidates for local, state, and federal offices are chosen in primary elections.

The winners of each party's primary election run against each other in the general election.

You can have a say in who your party's candidate will be by voting in the primary election.

Run-off Primary

Sometimes several people run for the same office in a primary election. When this happens, it is very hard for any one person to get a majority (over half) of the votes.

If no candidate wins a majority vote, the two candidates with the most votes have a run-off primary. The winner of the **run-off** primary runs in the general election.

General Election

The general election is the election in which the winners of each party's primary election run against each other to see who will be elected.

Voters from all political parties vote in the general election.

> State and national general elections are held the **first Tuesday in November in all even-numbered years.**

The President and Vice President, Congresspersons, governors, state senators and representatives, and many other state and county officials are elected in general elections.

Choosing Candidates for President

Choosing the candidates for President is not nearly as simple as choosing the candidates for other offices.

Presidential candidates are chosen by each political party at a **national convention**. These national conventions are held in the summer of every presidential election year.

Each political party sends **delegates** to their national convention to choose their party's candidate for President.

- In some states, convention delegates are chosen in party primaries.
- In other states, delegates are chosen by state party conventions.

Political Parties

The Two-Party System

The United States has a two-party political system.

The **Democratic** party and the **Republican** party are our two main political parties.

This system began early in our history. Remember the debate among the states in 1787 about approving the Constitution.

- The Federalists wanted a strong central government.
- The Anti-Federalists wanted the states to keep most powers of government.

Democrats

The **Democratic** party began as the Anti-Federalists. It supported strong state governments and a weak national government.

Later, the Democratic party became the party of the common people.

Before the Civil War, most Presidents were Democrats.

Republicans

The **Republican** party began in 1854. In the election of 1860, the Republican party opposed the expansion of slavery. Their candidate, Abraham Lincoln, was elected President.

After the Civil War, the Republican party was known as the party of the Union. From then until 1932, most Presidents were Republicans.

Since 1932, a Democrat has been elected President eight times and a Republican six times.

Minor Political Parties

Not all political candidates belong to one of the two major political parties.

In some local elections, members of minor political parties are elected to government offices.

The candidates of minor political parties usually don't expect to win national or even state elections. But these parties are still very important in the government of free people.

> **Minor** political parties are usually very concerned about **issues.**

The most important thing which minor political parties do is to raise issues which the major parties ignore.

The United States has had a variety of minor political parties.

Some issues which were first raised by minor political parties are:

- stopping slavery,
- stopping child labor,
- letting women vote, and
- making banks treat farmers fairly.

Later, all of these ideas were supported by major political parties. Now all of these ideas are part of our law. But the first political groups to raise these issues were minor political parties.

Think About It

1. What is the main way in which every citizen may have a say in government?
2. Who may vote in the United States?
3. Which groups of people could not vote when the Constitution was first written?
4. How did these groups get the right to vote?
5. Explain why a secret ballot is important in a democratic society.
6. What is lobbying?
7. What is the difference between a primary election, a run-off election, and a general election?
8. How are presidential candidates chosen?
9. Name the two major political parties in the United States today.
10. How did the Democratic party start?
11. How did the Republican party start?
12. What is the importance of minor political parties?

CHAPTER 31 *Paying for Governments*

It costs a lot of money to run each level of government—local governments, state governments, and the federal government.

> **Who pays the costs of governments?**
> The answer: **the people.**

Where the Money Comes from

Most of the money needed to pay the costs of government comes from taxes. Taxes are collected by all levels of government—by local governments, state governments, and the federal government.

Local Governments

Some taxes which **local governments** may have:

- **sales tax**—a tax on items people buy
- **personal income tax**—a tax on the money people earn from their jobs and the interest they receive from savings or investments. A local income tax is not very common. A local income tax is used mostly in large cities in states which have a state income tax.
- **property tax**—a tax on the property people own, including homes and businesses

Local governments also receive money from both state and federal governments. Some of the taxes which state and federal governments collect are sent back to local governments.

State Governments

Most state government money comes from taxes. Some taxes which state governments may have:

- **sales tax**—a tax on items people buy
- **personal income tax**—a tax on the money people earn from their jobs and the interest they receive from savings or investments
- **business taxes**—fees for business licenses, a tax on the income of businesses, and taxes on the removal of natural resources such as oil or timber
- **property tax**—a tax on the property people own
- **inheritance tax**—a tax on money or property which people inherit
- **gift tax**—a tax on large gifts of money or property

- **fees**—driver's license fees, motor vehicle registration fees, fees for recording legal documents

States get some money from insurance payments which employers pay for their employees. Unemployment insurance and workers' compensation are two such programs. Employers make payments into these insurance programs every month for each of their employees.

The state then uses the money in these insurance reserve funds to help workers who are unemployed or who are injured on the job.

States also receive money from the federal government. Part of the taxes which the federal government collects is returned to the states.

Federal Government

Some taxes the **federal government** collects:

- **personal income tax**—a tax which people pay on the money they earn and the interest they get from their savings
- **business income tax**—a tax on the income of businesses
- **social security tax**—a tax paid by workers and employers to pay for pensions of retired or disabled workers
- **excise tax**—a tax which people pay on such things as gasoline, liquor, and cigarettes
- **estate and gift taxes**—taxes people pay when they inherit money or property or when they receive large gifts
- **customs duties**—taxes collected on goods which are bought from other countries

- **unemployment insurance**—a tax paid by workers and employers to be used to help workers who are unemployed

Where the Money Goes

What happens to the taxes collected by governments?

Local Governments

Some ways that **local governments** spend their money:

- education
- health and hospitals
- public welfare
- sewage and sanitation
- streets and highways
- police protection
- fire protection

State Governments

Some ways that **state governments** spend their money:

- education
- health and hospitals
- public welfare
- highways
- insurance benefits
- grants to cities
- state highway patrol or state police
- conservation of natural resources
- commissions to regulate businesses and professions such as banking, insurance, transportation, medicine
- agencies to protect the rights of citizens

Federal Government

Some ways the **federal government** spends its money:

- public welfare
- health
- education
- veterans' benefits and services
- national defense
- interest on debt
- running national parks and national forests

Who Decides How the Money Will Be Spent?

At every level of government, elected officials decide how the government's money will be spent.

At the **local government** level, city council members, mayors, county commissioners, school board members, and other elected officials make most of the decisions about how local government money will be spent.

In **state governments**, members of the state legislature, state senators, and state governors decide how the state's money will be spent.

In the **federal government**, members of the House of Representatives, Senators, and the President decide how tax money will be spent.

What can the people do?

The taxes which support government are paid by the people. That includes you and your family.

> **Can you have a say in how governments spend your money?**
> The answer: **yes.**

You Can Vote

The first thing that you as a citizen can do is to help choose the members of your city, county, state, and federal governments.

To vote wisely, you must be informed. You must learn who is running for office, what each candidate thinks, and what issues are important to each candidate.

You Can Lobby

*Remember: **Lobbying** is writing or talking to people in the government to influence their decisions.*

Every citizen can lobby.

In your town or city or county, you can go to see your elected officials or telephone them at their offices. Tell them how you feel about important issues and why.

You can write letters to local, state, and federal government officials. It is especially helpful to write about an issue when it is being discussed by the decision makers. Explain how you would like the official to vote on the issue and why.

> To be a good lobbyist, you **must be informed.**

You Can Run for Office

Elected officials are people, just like you. They are men and women from all ethnic groups and many different backgrounds.

You, yourself, may want to run for political office some day.

The best way to prepare yourself for political office is to stay well informed about what is going on in your city and

153

county, in your state, in the United States, and in the world. It is also helpful to get a very good education.

Only a very small percentage of the American people will ever actually hold political office. But every citizen 18 years old and over can vote. Every citizen, no matter what age, can lobby. The way to make your government truly yours is to get involved.

Think About It

1. Who pays the costs of governments?
2. Name three kinds of taxes used by local governments.
3. Besides local taxes, where do local governments get money?
4. Name five kinds of taxes used by state governments.
5. Besides state taxes, where do state governments get money?
6. Name five kinds of taxes used by the federal government.
7. Name five ways local governments spend money.
8. Name five ways state governments spend money.
9. Name five ways the federal government spends money.
10. Who decides how government money will be spent at the local level? at the state level? at the federal level?
11. Explain how you can have a say in how your governments' money is spent.

CHAPTER 32
Influences on Your Political Beliefs

People have different political beliefs. How are people's political beliefs formed? What factors influence people's political beliefs?

Family and School

People's political beliefs are influenced by the beliefs of their families and the other groups to which they belong.

Most young children believe the same things their parents believe. Children hear their parents talking about political parties and candidates. To be like their parents, children may call themselves Democrats or Republicans even if they don't understand much about politics.

Children are also influenced by what they are taught in school. Children learn respect for the flag and the country in school. Later on students learn more about government and begin to examine issues and make judgments on their own. It is very important for citizens in a free society to be informed and make decisions based on facts.

Mass Media

Mass media refers to television, newspapers, magazines, radio. Public opinion is influenced by information presented in the mass media.

During political election campaigns, most candidates spend large sums of money buying television time and newspaper advertisements in order to get more votes.

Candidates may have television debates. They appear on talk shows and try to get as much news coverage as possible.

Most candidates believe that they will get more votes if more people hear about them.

Propaganda

Political ideas are influenced by **propaganda.**

Propaganda means ideas which are presented to influence people's opinions or behavior.

Propaganda appeals to people's fears and prejudices, not to their thinking. Propaganda uses emotionally-charged words and phrases rather than facts. Propaganda is used to advertise products as well as political candidates.

Some kinds of propaganda are:

- **Name calling**—calling a person some name in order to harm him or her. "Candidate X is un-American."
- **Glittering generalities**—using words which sound good but are vague or have little meaning. "Can

155

didate X is for freedom and justice." "This product has a miracle ingredient."

- **Bandwagon**—making people believe that everyone else is doing this. "Everyone in Yourtown is voting for Candidate X."
- **Testimonials**—people should support an idea because some famous person does. "I'm voting for Candidate X," says a famous movie actor.
- **Plain-folks**—making average people believe that a candidate is just like them. "Vote for me; I'm just a plain, hard-working person like you are."
- **Stacking the deck**—telling only part of the truth, exaggerating, bending the truth, oversimplifying an issue.

Propaganda influences voters who are not informed about the issues and candidates.

An informed voter can make a wise political choice based on facts and not be influenced by propaganda.

Think About It

1. How do families influence a person's political beliefs?
2. How are a person's political beliefs influenced by education?
3. What is the **mass media?**
4. Why do political candidates use the mass media?
5. What does **propaganda** mean?
6. Name four kinds of propaganda.
7. Why is it important to be informed about political issues and candidates?

UNIT G SUMMARY

Voting, lobbying, and running for political office are ways in which citizens can have a say in government.

Government officials are elected by secret ballots. Candidates for most offices are chosen in primary elections held by major political parties. Presidential candidates are chosen at national political party conventions. Most officials are elected in general elections held every two years.

Most state and national officials represent one of the two major political parties: Democrats or Republicans.

Minor political parties are also important to the government of free people. Minor parties support issues which major parties tend to ignore. Candidates of minor parties sometimes win local government offices.

The costs of government are paid by the people. Most money to run governments comes from taxes such as income tax, sales tax, property tax. Taxes are used to pay for education, health care, highways, police and fire protection, national defense, and other programs to benefit citizens.

Influences on people's political beliefs include the family, schools, mass media, and propaganda. By being well informed, citizens can make decisions based on facts, not propaganda.

UNIT G QUIZ

*Decide whether each statement below is **true** or **false**. Write **T** or **F** on your own paper. Then write a sentence which tells **why** each false statement is false.*

____ 1. The main way most people can have a say in government is by voting.

____ 2. In the United States today, voters must be at least 21 years old.

____ 3. Amendment 15 to the U.S. Constitution gave black men the right to vote.

____ 4. Amendment 19 to the U.S. Constitution gave women the right to vote.

____ 5. All elections in the United States today use a secret ballot.

____ 6. Lobbying means talking or writing to people to influence their decisions.

____ 7. In order to be a lobbyist, a person must be hired by an organization or large group.

____ 8. Candidates for local and state offices are chosen in primary elections.

____ 9. If no one candidate gets a majority in a primary election, a run-off primary is held.

____10. A general election is held every year in November.

____11. Candidates for President are chosen by national political party conventions.

____12. The two major political parties in the United States today are the Federalists and the Anti-Federalists.

____13. The Republican party was the first political party in the United States.

____14. The Democratic party is generally known as the party of the common people.

____15. Only members of a major political party can be elected to a government office.

____16. Minor political parties are usually concerned about issues which the major parties ignore.

___17. The issue of stopping slavery was first raised by a minor political party.

___18. The issue of letting women vote was first supported by a major political party.

___19. The costs of running governments are paid by the people.

___20. The only tax which most people ever pay is an income tax.

___21. Many state and local governments have a tax on property which people own.

___22. The federal government charges a fee for driver's licenses and automobile registrations.

___23. Customs duties are taxes paid on imported goods.

___24. Federal, state, and local governments spend money on education and health care.

___25. The President and Congress decide how tax money for all levels of government will be spent.

___26. There is no way for the average person to have a say in how tax money will be spent.

___27. Most children share their parents' political beliefs.

___28. Propaganda is used to appeal to people's emotions, not to their thinking.

___29. Telling only part of the truth is called the bandwagon technique.

___30. It is very important for all citizens in a free society to be well informed about political issues.

Learning Objectives for Unit H

When you have finished this unit, you will be able to:

- Describe the government of Britain today.

- Tell who runs the government of Britain.

- Explain some similarities between the British government and the U.S. government.

- Explain some differences between the British government and the U.S. government.

UNIT H

ANOTHER GOVERNMENT TODAY

In this Unit you will learn about the government in another important democracy, Great Britain. Great Britain and the United States have been close throughout history, but their governments function very differently.

BRITISH PARLIAMENT BUILDING
The Parliament Building (shown above) lies along the Thames River in London. The British Parliament is in some ways similar to the United States Congress. In this chapter you will learn how they are the same and how they are different.

The **United Kingdom**, or **U.K.** is the country that is made up of England, Scotland, Wales, and Northern Ireland. It is often referred to as **Britain**, or as **Great Britain**.

The government of Britain today is a **constitutional monarchy**. In some ways it is similar to the government of the United States. In other ways it is very different from the U.S. government.

Monarchy

One major difference between the government of Britain and the government of the United States is that Britain has a **monarch**. Queen Elizabeth II has been Britain's monarch since 1952.

In Britain today, the monarch has very little power. The Queen is mainly a symbol for the British people

Parliament

The government of Britain today us run by **Parliament**.

> *The word **parliament** means a government meeting at which people talk things over.*

In Unit A you learned that the nobles in England organized Parliament over 700 years ago to let the King know how the people felt.

At first Parliament had no real power. Parliament could give advice to the King, but the King didn't have to listen. Slowly Parliament gained more power.

Today Parliament runs the government of Britain.

The British Constitution

Britain's Constitution is not one single document.

Britain's Constitution is made up of

- important documents,
- laws passed by Parliament, and
- customs and traditions.

Documents

One of the important documents of Britain's Constitution is the **English Bill of Rights**. You learned about this document in Unit A.

The English Bill of Rights says that

- Monarchs can rule only if Parliament gives them this right.
- Anyone who is accused of a crime has the right to a trial by jury.
- People can petition the government if they believe the government has treated them unfairly.
- No punishment may be cruel or unusual.

- Fines for breaking the law must be fair.
- The monarch must follow the laws made by Parliament.
- Parliament must approve all taxes.

The English Bill of Rights is in some ways similar to the Bill of Rights in the U.S. Constitution.

Laws

The laws passed by Parliament are part of Britain's Constitution. These laws change from year to year. This means that Britain's Constitution is always changing.

Customs and Traditions

The customs and traditions which are part of the British Constitution include rules about how the government operates. This part of the British Constitution is not written down.

Comparing the U.S. and British Constitutions

You have learned that the U.S. Constitution is one single written document which has been changed very few times. All the laws of the United States are not part of the U.S. Constitution.

The British Constitution is different. Part of it is written down and part is not. Also, it changes from year to year. All of Britain's laws are part of its Constitution.

Organization of the British Government

Parliament

Parliament has the legislative, executive, and judicial powers of government in Great Britain.

Parliament has two houses:

- the **House of Commons** and
- the **House of Lords.**

The House of Commons has most of the power. The House of Lords has very little power.

House of Commons

Number of members—**635**
Members are called—**MPs**
Presiding officer—**Speaker of the House**

MP stands for **Member of Parliament.** MPs are elected by the voters and must be at least 21 years old. Their term of office is not set. However, elections must be held at least every five years. MPs are paid a salary for serving in Parliament.

The House of Commons is frequently called simply the **Commons.**

The House of Commons is the more powerful of the two houses of Parliament.

- Money bills must start in the Commons.
- A bill passed in the Commons may become law even if the House of Lords does not agree.

Most bills go through both houses of Parliament. However, if the House of Lords does not approve a bill, it can still become law if the Commons passes the same bill two years in a row.

163

House of Lords

Number of members—**over 1100**
Members are called—**Lords**
Presiding officer—**Lord Chancellor**

Members of the House of Lords include

- nobles who inherit their titles,
- archbishops and senior bishops of the Church of England, and
- life peers—people who are given noble rank for their lifetime.

Members of the House of Lords are **not elected** to office. The number of members changes over the years. Lords do not get paid for serving in Parliament.

The House of Lords has very little power in the British government. Some nobles with hereditary titles choose to give up their titles and run for seats in the House of Commons.

Fewer than 1/4 of all members of the House of Lords are actively involved.

Law Lords

A special group of the House of Lords, called the **Law Lords**, serve as the highest civil court for Great Britain and the highest criminal court for England and Wales.

Political Parties

Britain has two major political parties, —the **Conservative** party and the **Labour** party.

Britain also has minor political parties, including the **Liberal** party.

The leader of the party with the most members in Commons becomes the head of the government and is called the **Prime Minister.**

> **Remember:** In the British government, legislative, executive, and judicial powers are carried out by Parliament.

The Prime Minister is the chief executive official in the British government. Other executive officials, called **ministers**, are also chosen from members of Parliament. Together, these ministers form the **Cabinet.**

Ministers in the Cabinet come from both houses of Parliament, but the most powerful Cabinet offices are given to members of the House of Commons.

Judges of the lower courts in Britain are appointed by the ministers of the Cabinet.

The Government and the Opposition

The word **government** has a special meaning in Britain. The group of ministers who form the **Cabinet** are known as the **Government** (capital **G**).

After every election, a new Government is formed by the party with the most members in the House of Commons. If no one party has a majority, two or more parties get together and form a **Coalition** (joint) Government.

The party which has the second largest number of members in Commons is called the **Opposition.**

A Government lasts as long as it has a majority in Commons. It is possible for a Government to lose its majority at any time.

This can happen if

- members (MPs) who die or resign are replaced with MPs from another party,
- MPs from a minor party in a Coalition Government stop supporting the major party, or

- members of the Government party switch to the Opposition party.

Members of the House of Commons meet in a very large room which has five rows of benches on each side, facing each other. **Government** members sit on one side. **Opposition** members sit on the other side. MPs who are independent or members of minor parties may sit with either the Government or the Opposition.

Elections

MPs are the only members of the British government who are elected.

- Elections for MPs must be held at least every five years.
- Elections may be held more often than every five years.
- If a Government loses its majority, a new general election must be held.

The date of elections is set by the Prime Minister. Elections may be held at any time with 17 days' notice.

All British citizens who are at least 18 years old may vote, except for members of the House of Lords.

Think About It

1. What role does the monarch have in the British government today?
2. What group runs the government in Great Britain?
3. How is the British Constitution different from the U.S. Constitution?
4. What special meaning does the word Government have in Britain?
5. How are elections in Britain different from elections in the United States?

UNIT H SUMMARY

There are many forms of government in the world today. In this unit you have read about a form of government that is different from the United States government.

Britain

Britain is a constitutional monarchy with a symbolic monarch and a Parliament, which actually runs the government.

The British Constitution is not one written document. It is made up of important documents, laws passed by Parliament, and customs and traditions of the British people.

Parliament has two Houses: the House of Lords and the House of Commons.

Members of the House of Commons, called Members of Parliament, or MPs, are elected. The House of Commons is the more powerful of the two Houses of Parliament.

The House of Lords includes nobles who inherit their titles, high-ranking officials of the Church of England, and people who are given noble rank for their lifetime.

There are two major political parties in Britain and also some minor political parties.

Parliament controls the legislative, executive, and judicial functions of government. The leader of the political party with the largest number of members in the House of Commons is the chief executive official, called the Prime Minister. Other executive officials, called Cabinet Ministers, are chosen from the majority party. These ministers are known as the Government. The party with the second largest number of members in the House of Commons is called the Opposition.

Elections are held at least once every five years, but may be called at any time by the Prime Minister. All British citizens who are 18 years old or over, except members of the House of Lords, may vote.

UNIT H QUIZ

*Decide whether each statement below is **true** or **false**. Write **T** or **F** on your own paper. Then write a sentence which tells **why** each false statement is false.*

___ 1. Britain no longer has a monarch.

___ 2. The government of Britain today is run by Parliament.

___ 3. Britain's Constitution is a single written document.

___ 4. The English Bill of Rights guarantees a jury trial to people who are accused of a crime.

___ 5. Laws in Britain are passed by Parliament.

___ 6. The British Parliament has two houses.

___ 7. All members of the House of Lords have inherited titles.

___ 8. Members of the House of Lords are elected to office.

___ 9. Members of the House of Commons are called MPs.

___10. Members of the House of Commons are elected to office.

___11. Members of both the House of Lords and the House of Commons are paid a salary for serving in Parliament.

___12. The House of Lords is the most powerful house in Parliament.

___13. All bills must pass both the House of Lords and the House of Commons to become law in Britain.

___14. The chief executive official in the British government is called the President.

___15. The political party which has the largest number of members in the House of Commons controls the Government in Britain.

___16. In Britain, voters must be at least 21 years old.

___17. Elections in Britain are held regularly every four years.

Glossary

amendment—a change made in a constitution

anarchy—no government; everyone is free to do as they please

appeals court—a court which hears a case which has already been tried in a trial court

bill—a proposed law

bureaucracy—the departments of government which carry out the day-to-day business of government

candidate—a person running for political office

capitalism—an economic system based on the private ownership of the means of production

checks and balances—actions which each branch of government can take to stop or change actions of the other branches of government

civil case—a dispute about people's legal rights or duties

compromise—an arrangement in which everyone gets part of what they want and gives in a bit to what the others want

Congress—the lawmaking body of the federal government

constitution—a document which tells how a government will be run; it usually says who will choose the leaders, who will make the laws, who will carry out the laws, and how laws will be changed

contracts—agreements among people in which each person promises to do something or give something and expects to get something in return

criminal case—a court case in which the government accuses someone of breaking a criminal law

defendant—the person or group who is accused of doing something wrong

democracy—a government in which the people share in making the decisions

direct democracy—a government in which all the citizens take part in making the decisions and running the government

elastic clause—Article 1, Section 8, Clause 18 of the U.S. Constitution, which gives Congress the power to make laws which keep up with changing times

electors—people chosen by the political parties in each state to cast votes in the electoral college for president and vice president of the United States

executive branch—the branch of government which enforces the laws and runs the day-to-day affairs of government

exports—goods sent to another country

federal—a form of government in which a group of states join together and give some power to a central government; all the states are equal and all the states keep some power

felony—a major crime such as murder, rape, kidnapping, armed robbery, or arson

filibuster—a long talk for the purpose of stopping action on a bill

government—the way in which decisions are made for a group

grand jury—a group of citizens who decide if there is enough evidence against an accused person to hold a trial

impeachment—accusing a government official of some wrongdoing

imports—goods coming from another country

judgment—a court's decision in a civil case

judicial branch—the branch of government which decides if the laws are fair, decides if the laws have been broken, and settles problems which have to do with the laws

jurisdiction—the power of a court to hear a case

law—a rule which people must obey

legislative branch—the branch of government which makes the laws

lobbying—talking or writing to someone to influence his or her opinion

majority—over half

mass media—public information sources such as television, radio, newspapers, magazines

misdemeanor—a minor crime such as simple assault, trespassing, vagrancy

monarchy—a government in which the ruler is a person whose right to rule is inherited

oligarchy—a government in which a few people make the decisions and run the government

original jurisdiction—the right to hear a case for the first time

Parliament—a government meeting at which people talk things over

petit jury—a trial jury which decides if a defendant is innocent or guilty .

plaintiff—the person or group who takes a case to court

political party—a group of people who share similar political ideas and who support candidates from their group for public office

poll tax—a tax paid in order to vote

precedent—a decision which is later used to help make other similar decisions

primary election—an election to choose a party's candidate for the general election

ratify—to approve a treaty

real case—a case which has been brought to court and which involves a person actually breaking a law

representative democracy—a government in which citizens elect a few representatives to make the decisions and run the government

republic—a representative democracy

separation of powers—dividing the powers of government among more than one group or branch of government

social contract—an agreement among people about how the rules for their group will be made

tyrant—a cruel, unfair ruler

verdict—a court's decision in a criminal case

veto—to say no to a bill; to reject

zoning—dividing a city or county into areas based on how the land will be used

Index

A

Agnew, Spiro, 120
Amendments, 65-66, 67-70, 71, 72-75, 84, 97, 126, 136, 137
Anarchy, 16, 32, 50
Arrest, rights, 127, 136, 138
Articles of Confederation, 51-52, 55, 59
Assembly, 17

B

Bill of Rights
    English, 24, 25, 26, 162-63
    of state constitutions, 50, 56, 67
    of U.S. Constitution, 26, 56, 67-70, 127, 125, 136
Black people, 48, 73, 96
Britain, 42-46, 47, 51, 162-65 (*see also* England)
Brown v. Board of Education of Topeka, 137
Bureaucracy
    state and city, 104 *illus.*, 107
    federal, 109-11

C

Cabinet, 108, 109-10
    British, 164
Checks and balances, 96-98, 99, 111-12, 139, 140
Cities, 80-82, 99, 104
City manager, 104
City-states, 17
Civil cases, 128, 131,
Civil rights, 96, 137
Civil service examination, 100-01, 110

Code of Hammurabi, 13, 25, 26
Colonists, 42-46
Committees, legislative, 86, 87, 95
Compromise, 33, 55-56, 86, 87, 95, 97
Conference Committee, 86, 87, 94-95, 97, 99
Congress, 55, 65, 74, 88-98, 92 *illus.*, 99, 108, 111, 112, 113, 115, 120, 127, 132, 134, 139, 140
Constitutional Convention, 52 *illus.*, 52-53
    state, 66
Constitutions
    British, 162-63
    city, 80
    first among English settlers, 39-40
    first national constitution of U.S., 51-53
    state, 49-50, 57, 71, 83
    U.S., 54-56, 57, 63 *illus.*, 63-75, 79, 88, 89, 92-94, 96-98, 99, 113, 116, 117, 118-19, 127, 129, 132-39, 140, 145, 146
Contracts, 35-38, 128
    social contracts, 37-38, 40, 45, 50, 52, 56, 58
Counties, 80, 99, 104-05
Courts
    appeals, 129, 130, 131, 132-34
    federal, 74, 126, 132-38
    local, 130
    officers of, 126
    state, 74, 125 *illus.*, 126, 130-31
    trial, 125 *illus.*, 129, 130
    U.S. Supreme, 132-38
Criminal cases, 127, 128, 129, 131

D

Declaration of Independence, 43, 45-46, 47-48, 51, 58
Declaration of Rights, 44, 58
Defendant, 126-29, 139
Democracy, 16, 18, 33, 40, 162
   direct, 16, 17, 25, 38, 59
   representative, 16, 18, 25, 38, 40, 49, 54, 59
Democrats, 149-50
Departments
   city and county, 104
   federal executive, 109-10
   state, 90
Dictatorship, 16, 32
District Courts, 132
Due process of law, 68, 72, 127

E

Elastic Clause, 92
Election districts, 138
Elections, 80, 88, 90, 113-16, 146-50, 166
   British, 165
Electoral College, 74, 91, 114-16
England, 22-24, 25, 26, 35, 37, 42, 44, 136
   (*see also* Britain)
English Bill of Rights, 24, 25, 26, 162-63
Equal protection of the law, 74-75, 137
Executive branch of government, 49, 54, 65, 104-24
   federal, 108-21, 140
   local, 104-05
   state, 106-07
Executive departments, federal, 109-11

F

Felony, 109, 128
Ferraro, Geraldine, 119
Filibuster, 96
First Continental Congress, 44, 58

Ford, Gerald, 113, 120
Franklin, Benjamin, 53
Freedom
   from unreasonable searches and seizures, 68
   from cruel punishments, 69
   of religion, 50, 67, 136-37
   of speech, 50, 67, 135,
   of the press, 50, 67,
   to assemble, 50, 67,
   to keep weapons, 67
   to petition the government, 67
Fundamental Orders of Connecticut, 40, 58

G

Garner, John Nance, 114
Government of laws, 13, 49, 54, 101
Governments
   Ancient Greek, 17, 25,26
   Ancient Roman, 18, 25,26
   British, 162-65
   costs of, 151-54
   early governments in the New World, 35-41
   English, 22-24, 25
   federal, 18, 54, 64-75, 88-100, 108-21, 132-42, 152, 153
   forms of, 16, 32-33,
   Iroquois, 19-20, 25
   local, 18, 66, 80-82, 104-05, 130, 151, 152
   New England town, 18
   state, 18, 49-50, 54, 65, 79, 80, 83-87, 106-107, 131-32, 151, 152
Governor, 86, 87, 99, 106-07, 121, 126, 130, 149, 153
Grand jury, 68, 129
Great Britain, 42 (*see also* Britain)
Greece, 17, 25, 27, 48

H

Hammurabi, 13, 25
Hooker, Thomas, 39, 41 *illus.*, 41
House of Burgesses, 38, 58
House of Commons, 163-65
House of Lords, 163-65
House of Representatives, 55, 88-89,
    91-92, 94-99, 112, 139
Humphrey, Hubert, 114

I

Impeachment, 89, 91, 97, 98, 112-13, 120
Implied powers   *see* Elastic clause
Independent agencies, 110-11
Indians   *see* Native Americans
Iroquois Nation, 19-20, 25, 26

J

James I (King of England), 37
Jamestown, Virginia, 38
Jefferson, Thomas, 45, 48, 114
John (King of England), 22, 23
Johnson, Andrew, 112
Johnson, Lyndon, 113, 114
Judges, 97, 108, 125, 126, 130-40
Judgment, 128, 129
Judicial branch of government, 49, 54, 65,
    125 *illus.*, 125-40
    federal, 126, 129, 132-40
    local, 130
    state, 126, 129, 130-31
July 4, 1776, 45
Jury, 69, 127, 139
Justice of the Peace, 130

K

Kennedy, John, 97 *illus.*, 113, 119

L

Law Lords, 164

Laws
    British, 162-63
    civil, 69
    criminal, 69, 109
    equal protection of, 74-75, 137
    federal, 79, 88-98, 112-14, 119
    government of laws, 10, 13, 37, 41, 101
    local, 79, 81, 111
    state, 79, 83-87, 99, 105, 111
    written, 10, 13, 26, 27, 35, 40, 79
Legislative branch of government, 49, 54,
    55, 65, 79-99, 134, 142
    federal, 88-98, 142, 153
    local, 80-82, 153
    state, 83-87, 106, 138, 142, 153
    (*see also* Congress, House of Represen-
    tatives, Senate)
Lieutenant governor, 84, 106
Lincoln, Abraham, 112, 152
Lobbying, 148, 153
Lord Chancellor, 164

M

Madison, James, 53
Magna Charta, 22-23, 25, 26
Massachusetts Bay Colony, 39
Mayflower Compact, 37-38, 58, 57
Mayor, 104, 121, 153
Merit system, 110
Militias, state, 68
Miranda v. Arizona, 138
Misdemeanor, 128
Monarchy, 16, 22, 32, 162
MP (Member of Parliament), 163

N

National Guard, 68
Native Americans (Indians), 19-20, 25, 48
Nixon, Richard, 113, 120

O

Oligarchy, 33
One person, one vote, 95, 136, 138
Ordinances, 80, 130
Original jurisdiction, 130, 133
Override a veto, *see* Veto, override of

P

Pardon, 106, 108
Parliament, 23-24, 25, 26, 27, 35, 42, 44-46, 48, 162-65
Petit jury, 129
Pilgrims, 38, 58
Plaintiff, 126-28
Plural executive, 106-07
Plymouth, Massachusetts, 38
Pocket veto, 94
Politburo, 147
Political parties, 149-50, 157
Poll tax, 73
Popular vote, 115-17
Post Office (Postal Service), 92, 111
Preamble to the Constitution, 64
President of United States, 53, 65, 73, 74, 91, 94, 95, 97, 98, 108-21, 132, 133, 140, 143, 149, 150, 153
Primary election, 148-49
Prime Minister, British, 164
Prohibition, 72, 73
Propaganda, 155-56
Puritans, 39, 41 *illus.*

R

Reagan, Ronald, 117
Real cases, 134, 136, 139
Regulatory agencies, 110, 111
Reprieve, 108
Republic, 17, 18
Republicans, 149-50
Reynolds v. Sims, 138
Rockefeller, Nelson, 120

Rome, 11, 25, 27, 48
Run-off primary, 149

S

Schools, 137, 152, 153
    segregation in, 137
Second Continental Congress, 45, 51, 58, 59
Secret ballot, 18 *illus.*, 147-48
Self-determination, 72
Senate, 55, 74, 88, 89, 90-91, 94-98, 108, 110, 111, 112, 132, 133, 139, 139, 140, 153
Separation of church and state, 67, 136-37
Separation of powers, 26, 49, 79, 103, 134
Slavery, 65, 72, 73, 149, 150
Social contract, 37-38, 40, 45, 50, 52, 56, 58
Speaker of the House, 84, 88, 163
Supreme Court, U.S., 65, 68, 91, 97, 108, 112, 125 *illus.*, 132-38
    cases, 136-38

T

Taxation without representation, 44-45
Taxes, 22-23, 44-45, 47, 50, 51, 73, 74, 80, 89, 92, 93, 97, 136, 151-53
Town meetings, New England, 18
Treaties, 91, 97, 108, 133
Trial by jury, 24, 47, 50, 69, 127, 129, 162
Tyrant, 48

U

United Kingdom (UK), 162
United States of America (USA)
    creation of, 51

V

Verdict, 128, 129
Veto, 86, 94, 97, 106, 108, 112
    override of, 86, 94, 97, 112

Vice President, 73, 74, 90, 91, 112,
    113-14, 118, 119, 120
Voting, 18 *illus.*, 19, 21, 40, 44, 51, 73, 74,
    80-81, 83, 88, 90, 104, 106, 115-17, 138,
    146-50, 153, 157

W

Washington, George, 45, 52 *illus.*, 53, 58
Winner-take-all rule, 115
Women, 48, 73, 146

Z

Zoning, 82